Reclaiming Jesus

Making Sense of the Man
without the Miracles

Reclaiming Jesus

Making Sense of the Man
without the Miracles

Ian Breckenridge

BOOKS

Winchester, UK
Washington, USA

First published by O-Books, 2011
O Books is an imprint of John Hunt Publishing Ltd., The Bothy, Deershot Lodge, Park Lane, Ropley,
Hants, SO24 0BE, UK
office1@o-books.net
www.o-books.com

For distributor details and how to order please visit the 'Ordering' section on our website.

ISBN: 978 1 84694 414 7

Design: Tom Davies

Printed in the UK by CPI Antony Rowe, Chippenham, Wiltshire
Printed in the USA by Offset Paperback Mfrs, Inc

We operate a distinctive and ethical publishing philosophy in all
areas of its business, from its global network of authors to
production and worldwide distribution.

CONTENTS

He went round to all the people
A paper crown on his head.
Here is some bread from my father.
Take, eat, he said.

Nobody seemed very hungry.
Nobody seemed to care.
Nobody saw the god in himself
Quietly standing there.

He finished up in the papers.
He came to a very bad end.
He was charged with bringing the living to life.
No man was that prisoner's friend.
Charles Causley, Ballad of the Bread Man

For Elaine and Gillian

Acknowledgments

Writing this book has been by turns rewarding and challenging, obliging me to think through, question and fill out all kinds of detail along the way. It has been a learning curve like no other, changing my view significantly on a number of issues.

I owe a debt to many writers from whom I have learned over the last decade or two about the subjects touched on in this book, and many of these are mentioned in the list of sources. I apologize for what some authors might see on occasion as a misunderstanding or misrepresentation of their words – the mistakes are mine.

Closer to home, I am especially indebted to the Friends in the Norwich Quaker Meeting, whose influence has shaped me imperceptibly over the years, and who incidentally keep a splendid, very up-to-date small library which I have used extensively. Over the past fifteen or so years I have also been grateful for many insights gained at meetings of the Norfolk Theological Society and of Kaleidoscope, until recently a well-named inter-church group based in Norwich.

In more recent years I was much influenced by Rex Ambler's remarkable insights into early Quaker practice, and thereby helped to see more clearly the inner life of the Kingdom. In the past few years I have been indebted to my daughter Gillian for several theological conversations arising out of her own studies at Edinburgh University and at Union Seminary in New York. In the spring of 2004 I attended a course at King's Lynn Meeting House, 'Rooted in Christianity, Open to New Light', led by Tim Peat Ashworth and Alex Wildwood for Woodbrooke, the Quaker Study Centre. This course was one factor encouraging me to set out on the adventure of writing this book.

My thanks especially to Brian Thorne and also to Harvey Gillman and Hilary Wakeman for the support and sometimes candid advice which they gave during the process of writing the book. My thanks also to Alan Berry, Rodney Hooper, Dori Veness, Alan Webster and Nigel Wimhurst for insight and inspiration relating to various themes in the book; to Justin Barnard, Toni Berry, Joe Daines, Ian Galliford, Meg Hull, Barbara Mitchels and Sylvia Stevens for encouragement and feedback as the chapters emerged; to Lucy Parker for her unfailing knowledge of computer software, and to Evelyn Woodcock for proofreading and advice on layout.

Even closer to home, I am indebted to my brother George for the many years of dialogue and debate which have helped shape my views today. I will always be grateful for the love and support of my family down the years: Pamela, Elaine and Gillian, and to Beryl for her love and support in more recent years. Finally I owe a debt to my parents, who did me the incomparable favor of setting me out on this journey in the first place, even if they couldn't have foreseen where it would take me.

I have been moved and inspired by this man who has come out to me from the biblical record and whom I have learned to know so very much better than I had ever done before. Frankly I have been more impressed than I expected to be. I cannot help but admire the searching psychological depth and the sheer originality of his thinking, bringing to life a powerful new reality in the mind. Equally I am surprised by the warmth and energy of the larger-than-life personality which has emerged.

Still, the position I have reached today is essentially provisional, a way marker on a journey, a distinctive understanding within a profound surrounding mystery. I am grateful for this understanding, this glimpse, and now more than ever I look forward to further intriguing surprises on the way ahead.

Unless otherwise stated, all biblical quotes are from the Revised English Bible

Introduction
The Point about Jesus

How can we understand this figure from another time in history? Is it possible to get inside the head of someone from another culture which is so foreign to us? Some would say that this is simply not possible, and that the best we can do is recreate something of his world using the words and assumptions of our own time. But can we do even this? Can we sum up the vision which he saw then, in words that make sense to us now? Even this could be difficult in the case of someone like Jesus who has aroused so many conflicting responses.

It does seem that often vicious controversy engulfed him in his own lifetime and has never really left him in the centuries since then. For someone who is seen as a man of peace, this is bizarre. Could it be that it is too simple to call him a man of peace? Why did so much furious and indeed murderous controversy surround him? Was there something about him which provoked this violent response in some people? Was there something important at stake, something which perhaps eludes us today?

Is there a key which can help us here? Can we find one theme which can sum up for us today what this classical era teacher is all about? Some have pointed to a feature which seems to underlie all his teaching: an intuition that, deep down underneath surface appearances, human nature is in some kind of exile or imprisonment, constantly looking round for some kind of homecoming, some kind of liberation. 'Exile?' we might say, scratching our twenty-first century heads. 'Exile from what, exactly?' Here we are again, with a logic and a vision from another time. How can we make sense of this today?

It's true that human beings as a species do need to make sense of their world and their own place in it; indeed this seems to be one of the most basic traits which define our humanity. It's also true that unfortunately, a lot of the time, our experience of life stubbornly fails to make enough sense. The problem is that we seem to need to see at least enough sense in things to make it worth while to keep the quest going. This makes this quest unstable and unpredictable, a crucial but high-risk undertaking which people can easily be tempted to give up. Unable to make any kind of sense of themselves, they may not find much value in themselves either, and low self-esteem does seem to follow a lot of people like a shadow through much of their lives. Sometimes, indeed, this can spark violence.

Today this can either drive us into some comforting but unreal fantasy world, or make us build up a cynical, perhaps aggressive exterior shell behind which we can hide, sometimes concealing symptoms of quiet despair. Of course things are often not as bad as that, and we can find consolation and inspiration from many sources, but nevertheless this darker side of the picture can probably ring true for most of us to some degree for some of the time. As a species, we are created to find meaning and worth, and some of the time we just don't manage to find it. Expressed in other words, you could say that we find ourselves in some degree of underlying distress, perhaps of alone-ness and pointlessness, a degree of exile from our own surrounding reality and indeed from ourselves. The thing we need to know most of all, it seems, is who on earth we are.

This does appear to be the underlying human dilemma which Jesus seems to have put his finger on, something in the human condition which can stir deep fears and longings. That may be one reason why he has provoked such diverse reactions, some of them violent, and that, in a nutshell, may be why he is worth our attention today.

Sometimes this man speaks the language and expresses the preoccupations of his own age, but at other times he does appear to be speaking a universal language to people in all ages. So sometimes he will sound utterly strange, while at other times he will reach out and touch a point right inside us. This contrast, this alternating strangeness and startling familiarity, will surface from time to time throughout this book.

Reasons for Reopening the File

Today we see Jesus through the haze and the distorting mirrors of 2,000 years of history. The figure we see reflects in part the understanding of late classical Greek minds, often hard won following bitter dispute. On top of this, today's figure no doubt also reflects the needs and priorities of an alliance of church and political hierarchies which has endured through many centuries. We sense that this strange image which we have of Jesus today is in some ways no longer authentic. Perhaps we need to try to clear the haze, to see past the distorting mirrors.

Not surprisingly, people today see him in many different ways. For some people he is nothing less than God the Son 'to earth come down', and this can make it really quite hard to see him as a human being at all. Some of these people may indeed be pretty uncomfortable with the very idea of revising their picture of Jesus, perhaps afraid that to do so might in some way diminish it – the idea that it might enhance it perhaps has not occurred to them. For others he may be an inspiring teacher of the enduring power of love in human affairs; for others again, he is the menacing judge of all the earth; while for a good many others he is a discredited irrelevance, a man who can walk on water, a bit of a joke figure at best. For most of us, I suspect, he is a somewhat incoherent patchwork of all of these.

Yet underneath all this, there is evidence which shows us another figure, a larger-than-life figure who sees the possibility of an experience of living which is free from precisely this obsession with death and gloom. This man senses a paradox right at the heart of human nature, and again and again in his stories he turns our expected world upside down. He is a most radical and profound skeptic of human power, money and political vainglory, seeing through all this, sensing underneath it a discomfort and a distress deep in the human heart. He seems to see underneath the surface of things.

His vision mixes ideas like sickness and healing, blindness and seeing, exile and homecoming, liberation and the exhilaration of life renewed. Metaphor and paradox mix freely as he imagines a Kingdom within us which reverses ordinary human logic. What can he do with such an anarchic tumult of inspiration but challenge us to make our own sense of it? If this is a light within us, after all, he is confident that we will see it sooner or later.

It is really quite strange, though, that for so very many people in our time Jesus has simply ceased to mean anything at all. A figure which once defined and bestrode a whole civilization appears to have vanished almost entirely from the awareness of a great many people. This book starts with this puzzle and wonders how it came about.

When we look for an underlying cause, it would be very easy to point to a frantic, neurotic culture and to claim that the modern Christian faith itself is essentially blameless, but this seems implausible. For a generation and more, there has been ample evidence around us of a search for a credible basis for living, but until very recently this search has, for large numbers of people, strangely bypassed churches, certainly in Europe.

There are those who fear that this may be a symptom of a more serious underlying situation, as all world cultures are cast adrift from more and more of their roots amid an accelerating pace of enveloping, ubiquitous change. In the century just finished, a headless nationalism and two brutal post-Christian ideologies, both in part symptoms of a rootless culture, have already led to worldwide catastrophe and a series of unspeakable events. This is hardly an encouraging preparation as, alongside

4

today's rising hopes and aspirations, our world now faces crises which are simply unprecedented in their scale and in the depth of the challenge they pose. At times it does seem that human nature may be irredeemably, perhaps suicidally flawed. Can we as a species manage to survive at all?

Perhaps we all need to dig deeper and very deliberately into the roots of our own fractured culture if we are to find the wisdom required to navigate safely through this new set of challenges. As part of this digging deeper we might examine why this once dominant faith seems now to be so burdened by a disabling credibility problem, certainly in the eyes of many onlookers and some insiders. This modern stand-off with the sciences and to some degree with a whole surrounding culture was not built into Christianity when it began. Can we restate Jesus' teaching in a way which sidesteps this whole mismatch?

This book will try to get underneath the unreal travesty of Jesus which survives in the minds of many people today. It will seek out a more authentic figure, will piece together different strands of logic in his teaching and will see what they might add up to. It does seem possible that this Iron Age thinker can speak to this still newly affluent age in a way which is deeply skeptical yet also ultimately optimistic.

One immediate problem is that we may not be able to hear Jesus properly above the noise and confusion of traditional church stereotypes, ideas expressed in this arcane language from another age. So it might in fact be useful to create a picture of him which is free of this confusion and these stereotypes as far as we can make it, a picture which lets him speak directly to us again in a language which reflects the way we experience our own world. This book will try to do just that.

Writing this Book

Some years ago I set out on a learning adventure, aiming to come to a deeper understanding of a faith with which I had been brought up, which I then rejected and then still later came back to. This faith, it seemed to me, finally deserved a degree of uninterrupted, consistent attention over a period of time similar to that which I might devote to a course of academic study. Very soon the adventure became deeper, wider and more exhilarating than I had expected, an enthusiastic response to the great gift of life itself. Since then it has frequently bowled me over, on several occasions leading me to conclusions which took me by surprise.

I learned a new respect for the sophistication and subtlety of Jesus' teaching, the so-called Kingdom teaching. It is true that some of the strands in this teaching no longer speak to us today. For example, Jesus sometimes does seem to expect that history is about to come to a climax, a cataclysm in which the Roman power will be swept away. It is also true that the teaching as a whole is not immediately accessible – none of the four Bible narratives sets it out at any point as one single coherent system. But I soon realized that, despite all this, the themes in this teaching hang together remarkably well and have evidently been thought through in some detail. Whoever this thinker was, he has evidently meditated deeply on his subject. This Kingdom of Heaven he speaks of is apparently an inner realm within each of us, in some sense born in us, which can heal us, reconcile us with each other and finally dissolve our sense of exile from the creation which gave us birth. This is quite a claim.

The other thing that struck me about this teaching is how complete it is in itself. Later doctrines may or may not enhance it, but it doesn't actually need them to shore it up or complete it. This gives us a foundation on which to re-explore the entire Christian faith, going right back to its roots. Soon the picture emerges of a still-young man, influenced by some of the movements of his day, bringing together his own insights in a learning process which appears to deepen rapidly over a quite short period of time. He is inspired by this experience; he is filled with enthusiasm, fired by anger and driven by raw compassion, and all of this urgency and enthusiasm fairly spill over onto the text.

For many people today, Christian belief is a confusing jungle with all kinds of unexplained and sometimes frankly implausible loose ends. I hope that this book will at the very least cut through some of this jungle and let in some light. I hope that it will also uncover some of the human logic and emotional power which attracted people to this teaching originally. This is the reason why the book will try to avoid traditional words as far as possible, and to find an authenticity true to Jesus' own time, bypassing the backward-looking logic which seems to attach to the Christian faith today.

People are by now aware of the truly awesome nature of the challenges which we now face as a species. Perhaps our current obsession with materialism is a symptom of a deeper unease. How can life possibly be full, we ask ourselves, unless we continue to consume at our present rate? Voices from our tradition gently say it can actually be fuller than it is now without this obsession, but most of the time I suspect that we just don't dare to trust them. And guess who just might be one of our more perceptive commentators on that very theme? Quite possibly the man who is the subject of this book. Maybe he deserves our attention for that reason alone.

Still, I do need to be especially clear about what I am proposing to undertake here. I will need to navigate between several dangers. For example, among the many attempts in modern times to depict a 'historical' Jesus, quite a few have turned out to be more a Jesus who reflects the author's personal preoccupations or values: Jesus the social revolutionary, Jesus the mystic, and so on. Quite a few other accounts have been in effect 'Jesus novels', a good read perhaps, but with a pretty tenuous historical authority. A further genre in recent years has been that of 'hard-hitting' investigative journalism, uncovering 'sensational' new facts, the kind of (alleged) non-fiction you might find in an airport bookstall.

For most of the last century, indeed, some theologians have tried to get on with constructing a Christ of faith without examining his historical roots too closely. But this project in turn seemed beset with its own difficulties. There did seem to be a figure, referred to strikingly by some as the pre-Christian Jesus, awkwardly lurking there in the evidence and he could not easily be finessed away.

So we do have to pay close attention to the evidence, but if we do this we may then run into the opposite danger of being historically accurate but bloodless. It is possible to write about Jesus and fail entirely to convey the extraordinarily subversive challenge to all of us contained in his teaching. I suppose what I'm trying to do is something in-between some of these other approaches: an account which respects historical evidence but also judiciously applies a modicum of historical imagination to it, trying to get to the heart of this story and bring it to life. This also means restoring a picture of Jesus' full humanity in terms we can understand in our own time. Like the late first-century Gospel writers, maybe we too need to recall the memory of the man himself, the man whose extraordinary vision set the whole thing running.

I am aware of my own limits but grateful for different influences on me. The influence of the Quaker community, to which I now belong, can be recognized at many places throughout the book. Traces of my evangelical childhood still remain, including some of its enthusiasm and emotional appeal. Equally, the more skeptical tone of many years as an agnostic will also come to the surface. The enthusiasm and the skepticism are both authentic. More occasional influences from other religions can also be seen at various points.

Perhaps above all, I hope to avoid polemical certainty. Behind it all, I need to remember that I'm dealing here with the inexpressible mystery and grandeur of existence. Weaving my way through this, I hope to create a portrait of Jesus which comes convincingly alive and speaks to people today with a fresh voice.

A Glance through the Book

Right at the start this book identifies some of the sources of confusion about Jesus in modern minds, and attempts to lay bare some historical roots of the mismatch, the degree of alienation which has arisen between faith and culture. Having done this, it then explores the evidence on which we might build a fresh picture of Jesus, his human achievement, and his relation to the faith which arose in response to him.

Building on this foundation, the book then lays out at some length Jesus' central vision of a Kingdom of Heaven, an inner reality, truly a kingdom of the heart within each of us, yet also alive among us, capable of igniting in us a lively hope for the future. The book then meditates on the extraordinary events of the passion narratives, trying to see them through the lens of the vision and teaching which preceded them. It then goes on to investigate a few of the major turning points in Christian history, seeing them again through this same lens of Jesus' original teaching, and this eventually brings us back to the curious situation of the modern faith which the book started with.

While doing all this, the book has been building up a portrait of Jesus in his own time which pieces together some of the underlying logic of his vision, where it came from and the stages which it may have gone through. It points to evidence of his background and early experience, elements of his personality, his way of seeing the world, his way of relating to people, and snatches of his vocabulary and characteristic turns of phrase.

After this the book goes back to Jesus' own distinctive vision of his God, seeing strands of perhaps unexpected logic in it, and later (in an appendix) looks at the later doctrine of the Trinity, how it arose, and what it might possibly mean to us today. The book then ponders ways beyond the present impasse attaching to the Christian faith, ways of re-understanding and reconfig-uring the core of this faith which can then speak directly to people in our own time again. It then goes on to consider what Jesus may have to say to humanity as a whole as it faces the specific challenges of the twenty-first century. The book finally comes back to the man whose wholly unexpected vision set this whole thing in motion, concluding with an outline portrait of a figure which can still surprise and intrigue.

Jesus holds up a mirror to us, allowing us to see ourselves in a new perspective, taking us beyond our familiar social context and setting us firmly within the framework of the great creation itself. Can this inspire us as a species to do what we need to do to survive?

Ian Breckenridge

Norwich

October 2009

Part One
A Quest for an Authentic Jesus

Part One first draws attention to a number of puzzles, among them the unreal and contradictory images of Jesus current today and the wider discomfort of the modern Christian faith in its surrounding culture. It wonders if we might understand Jesus better if we lay aside the assumptions of later history and go back to the evidence. It then takes a few bearings and sets a few perspectives before setting out.

Chapter 2 then examines the evidential basis for a new picture of Jesus. It considers the evidence for and against Jesus' existence, and then goes on to examine the mixture of legend and authenticity in the four biblical narratives. It then discusses some limits imposed by cultural distance, and the need to sift this teaching in order to see within it what can speak to us today. Chapter 3 brings the evidence together and assesses what kind of conclusions it permits us to draw. It then presents the first sketches of Jesus, which will build up to a fuller portrait later in the book.

If you wish, you may prefer to omit the essentially preliminary issues in Chapter 2, and proceed to Chapter 3, where the portrait of Jesus begins. Or you may prefer to move on directly to Part Two of the book, where a series of seven chapters examines Jesus' central teaching about an inner Kingdom.

Chapter 1
Something's Not Right

Contradictory Images

The following anecdote was doing the rounds recently. I heard it as a report of an actual conversation overheard on a street corner between two young women. It ran something like this: 'I like your cross; it definitely suits you. [Pause] I've got one quite like it, only mine's got a little man on it.' It seems this was not meant as a joke but was said in all innocence. This young woman had no idea who the figure on her cross was meant to represent.

Jesus is vanishing before our very eyes, perhaps because the different figures we have of him have by now so very little meaning for people, so little connection with the world they live in. For some people he's the man in the blond hippy beard and the white robe preaching soft-focus goodness, the Bambi Jesus surrounded by toddlers and bunny rabbits, remembered here and there in portraits on the walls of some church vestries and annexes. Others see him in somewhat darker tones as the ultimate authority figure, the 'pale Galilean', unsmiling, death-obsessed, God play-acting the role of a human being. This figure is maybe seen as strict and rejecting to people like divorcees and gay people who fail to come up to his high standards of perfection.

For others again, Jesus is just a minor figure of fun, nothing more than a cue for a joke about loaves and fishes perhaps. And for plenty of others his name survives simply as a meaningless exclamation, an expletive vaguely expressing indignation or even just mild surprise! The idea of taking Jesus seriously would strike quite a few people today as surprising and at first sight perhaps quite amusing.

Yet for us in our Prozac society there are other sides to this

13

man's teaching which can still move us. He takes a deliberate stance on the side of the poor and of those whom the rest of us barely notice. He mocks hypocrisy and condemns the complacent heartlessness of those in authority. He speaks in lyrical terms of the generous beauty of the creation. Somehow in modern times this altogether more appealing figure of Jesus has become confused with the ludicrous Bambi figure. Has the other figure, the solemn church establishment figure, survived more clearly in the public imagination? It's hard to say, but surely it is the confusing mixture of these two parodies of Jesus which people cannot bring themselves to take seriously today.

These two figures could, moreover, amount to a serious libel on the third figure: the friend of the outcasts and the harsh critic of all power establishments. This situation is very strange indeed when we think about it. Does this other, rapidly vanishing Jesus deserve more of our attention? Can we reassemble some authentic understanding of him before he vanishes entirely?

Many people think that the current confusing images of Jesus are derived from the Bible, rather than reflecting the many centuries of church authority since it was written. In fact the four narrative accounts of Jesus found in the Bible, put together long before the emergence of this authority, reveal someone far removed from the images which we have inherited.

Here is a first glimpse. The following extract from one of his most celebrated stories can give us a flavor of how he saw things.

There was once a man who had two sons; and the younger said to his father, 'Father, give me my share of the property.' So he divided his estate between them. A few days later the younger son turned the whole of his share into cash and left home for a distant country, where he squandered it in dissolute living. He had spent it all when a severe famine fell upon that country and he began to be in need ... Then he came to his senses: 'How many of my father's hired servants have more food than they can eat,' he said, 'and here am I, starving to death! I will go at once to my father, and say to him "Father, I have sinned against God and against you; I am no longer fit to be called your son; Treat me as one of your hired servants."' So he set out for his father's house.

But while he was still a long way off his father saw him, and his heart went out to him; he ran to meet him, flung his arms round him, and kissed him. The son said, 'Father, I have sinned against God and against you; I am no longer fit to be called your son.' But the father said to his servants, 'Quick! Fetch a robe, the best we have, and put it on him; put a ring on his finger and sandals on his feet. Bring the fatted calf and kill it, and let us celebrate with a feast. For this son of mine was dead and has come back to life; he was lost and is found.' And the festivities began.[1]

Whatever you make of the idea of God, Jesus certainly stands on its head the historical picture of an august, distant creator which was so often favored and projected by a later church. The God of Jesus sees you while you are still a long way off; his heart goes out to you and he quite forgets himself, running out to meet you, flinging his arms around you and kissing you as his lost child. Where is the stern authority figure here? This God doesn't frown or scold you or comment on what you've done. How can he do this when he is so overjoyed at finding you again? Notice that this God also gives you more than you had ever thought of asking for. He is the home which you left, and come back to. And when you do come back, the festivities begin!

Feasting is a recurring motif in the four narrative Gospels. Time and again Jesus is pictured eating and drinking with others, people at all levels of society, celebrating together with them. Feasting and celebration do seem to be at the heart of this message. Again it occurs to us that this heart of the message may have been somehow overlain, or diluted, or finessed into something else. How was it changed, and why did people want to change it?

The puzzle deepens. This gentle teacher of non-violence and the healing of the human heart is executed in bizarre circumstances and for reasons which seem frankly unconvincing. What is behind this? Clues there are in plenty, but can we read them in a way that makes sense of them? Fast-forward several centuries and the image of this man has been altered quite beyond recognition, made into the king above earthly kings and the wrathful judge of all wrongdoers. What mixture of motives could have brought people to preside over this veritable character assassination?

All this, moreover, seems to culminate in one final, overarching puzzle. If Christianity was a dominant belief system for so long, why in modern Europe has its influence very nearly disappeared altogether? Why, for so many people, has Jesus to all intents and purposes simply vanished? Among many people today, for example, ideas of God and of the supernatural seem not just on balance implausible but simply incomprehensible. This gospel is no longer self-evident. How has this come about? By now we are looking at the alienation of a whole religious faith from its surrounding culture, a rift which in some ways defines modern times.

A Confusing Legacy

There was a time in its early centuries when the Christian faith spoke to its own culture with authentic power, speaking the language of its own time. Many centuries later in a very different world, it seems to cling to the world from which it came. Magic and miracle, for example, were very much a part of the world in which people of that time lived every day. Now the continued use of this kind of language can easily persuade onlookers that this is a faith firmly rooted in a past which is long gone, rather than in the vividness of present experience and the inspiration of future hope.

As we have seen, the picture of Jesus we have inherited from the last 2,000 years is in any case a strange jumble of images, everything from 'gentle Jesus, meek and mild' to the stern judge of all the earth. But the problem is more than just one of confusion; there is a dark side to this too. My own childhood was dominated by a very particular image of Jesus, and as a small boy it was hard for me to escape its baleful presence. The bottom line with this Jesus was that you had to believe in him or you would burn in the lake of fire for the rest of time. People said that God loved us, and that we could escape his wrath by simply accepting this love, but what on earth could we have done to deserve this kind of response, and what kind of love could contemplate punishing people so fearfully for the crime of not believing?

Even stranger, I was asked to believe that Jesus was somehow actually a part of God. As the carol says:

He came down to earth from heaven,
Who is God and Lord of all[2] ...

With the best will in the world this sounds to modern ears like space invaders, making Jesus into a strange kind of hybrid creature. In fact this kind of confusing picture has created all kinds of problems for modern minds. Somewhere in my late teen years all these miracles – water into wine, virgin birth and all that – well, they seemed simply unworthy of belief.

Yet this situation leaves other people dissatisfied, feeling that in this brave new religionless world Jesus may have been dismissed too easily. Jesus for many people today is an anchor, a source of reassurance in a complex, unsettling world, while for others he is an inspiration, giving to life a beauty and a depth it otherwise wouldn't have. So how can we respond to this? Can we reinterpret some of the more implausible elements in the story as myth, symbolic stories expressing the truth of the heart in a similar way to great fiction? Are some of the more unattractive traits due simply to the distortions of history? Perhaps time itself obscures the clarity of all original vision, piling complication on complication, obscuring the force of its original impact.

Hindsight and the Appeal to Authority

Many church people tend to respond to this with an appeal to authority, whether of the Bible or of church tradition, but this tends to leave the wider non-Christian public largely unimpressed. Isn't relying on authority to back up your beliefs perhaps a bit too easy? More than this, might it even at times have subtly distorted the truth we thought we believed? Historically has it not done much to project an image of Jesus as a stern figure who commands, crowding out the healer, the gentle friend of the friendless? Where is the God who patiently wins our confidence and dares us to love with all our heart?

After many centuries this had perhaps become a faith which saw its origins through the glass of later historical authority and found itself slipping little by little into a very human hindsight logic. According to this logic, Jesus can save us because he is God (and not the other way round), and we should believe this because it has the guarantee of God's personal authority (and no longer principally because it can fire the heart with its beauty). In this way a gap of mutual incomprehension has opened up between Christian people and those around them. In a real sense they now live in different worlds.

If Jesus has to be accepted as God without further comment or qualification right at the start, this can have the effect of freezing any chance of honest discussion. Likewise if Jesus is seen as in some way perfect, it can be difficult to see him as a real human being. In fact the image we have of him by now may have lost some of its ring of authenticity and have become strangely two-dimensional. But if we can manage to put to one side the superstructure of authority and perfection, then we may be able to bring this figure more convincingly alive again. Paradoxically it may be helpful to suspend for a time the claim that he is divine, look at the man again with fresh eyes, and then see more clearly why people came to this conclusion about him. Then we too might see more clearly what was humanly appealing about him.

Where can we find a solid basis for truth outside traditional authority? I think we may find it in the same place as people did 2,000 years ago: among those who listened to Jesus. Does it speak to the heart? If it does, listen to it, trust it as far as you can, and follow where it will lead you.

Taking our Bearings

This book is aware of the marvelous awakening in our own time to the awesome scale and detail of our surrounding creation. Discoveries made in various fields of science during the past half-century, from the Big Bang to the genome, from the origins of our own species to the remarkable secret life of the brain, are of a transforming scale and significance. Indeed it's hard to see how they can fail to influence the ways in which people see themselves. Who knows, this may yet change the whole meaning of a religious faith by the end of the century we have just begun.

This book also understands Christianity as one among several religious traditions in our shrinking world, each with its own internal legitimacy, and doesn't hesitate to make comparisons between them.

A comment about the use of the word 'God' in this book. For me this one word sums up the intimate immensity in which we live and move and have our being, wholly out-scaling us and yet closer to us than breathing, a Reality to which we are umbilically joined. In this book I do retain the convention of using the pronoun 'he' (and also incidentally a capital 'G'), but not because God can ever be bound by the limits of a quasi-human personality, let alone those of masculinity. This would surely be an elementary and indeed comical misunderstanding when we are trying to express the mystery and the dazzling glory of existence itself. Incidentally I am also careful to refer, not to Jesus' experience of God per se, but of *his* God, his own particular understanding of God.

I do find it hard to distinguish between God and the universe, between creator and creation. To conceive of God without the creation seems to me entirely futile and without meaning. This astonishing, inspiring universe has been referred to as his handiwork, his signature, his dance, even his autobiography. All these metaphors have their place, and they do remind us that religious language is necessarily imaginative and imprecise, in some ways akin to the language of poetry.

This faith does rest on a teaching about sickness and healing, about dying, trusting and letting go, and about new life springing up eternally within us. These are powerful metaphors. Maybe there are depths under the surface of conventional twenty-first century Christianity and if we trust enough to dig down we may find foundations which turn out to be stronger than the ones many people rely on today. Who knows, we may even rediscover a comprehensive 'faith of all truth', once again embracing both imagination and reason, poetry and science. In this day and age, indeed, perhaps nothing less will do.

Experts seem to be reaching a consensus that our own species has been around on this earth for anything between 150,000 and 200,000 years, depending on the point at which you start counting. Our recent cousin *Homo erectus* seems to have survived for rather longer, well over a million years in fact. If we can now find a way through the major crises of our own time, there is no saying for how many more millennia our species can survive and thrive together and cherish this planet and celebrate the sacred gift of life. It's a big 'if'. But if we do manage to survive, we will have put this present age of fear and greed and violence well behind us.

Chapter 2
Setting Out on the Quest

Did He Really Exist ?

In the case of some very influential historical characters there is really very little indeed that we actually know about them. Lao Tzu, the founder of Taoism in ancient China, is one such case in point. What we know about Socrates is almost all conveyed in the writings of Plato and Xenophon, but few people would seriously argue that Socrates was no more than a figment of their imagination. Plato and Xenophon were pupils of Socrates and knew him well. However, people do build legends because they need to believe in them. Did King Arthur really exist, or is he a conflation of several different historical characters? This is how some legends grow over time.

In the case of Jesus some experts argue that we actually have quite a lot of reasonable quality evidence, although the effect of legend formation can also be detected in the biblical record.[3] The four New Testament Gospels are a frankly enthusiastic series of apologias written some decades after Jesus died, but it does seem that the sources of some pieces of their narrative are probably much closer to the source, on occasion even first-hand or very close to it. One of the narrators, Luke, expressly states that he has 'investigated the whole course of these events in detail' in order to produce 'an orderly narrative' providing 'authentic knowledge', and that he is 'following the traditions handed down to us by the original eyewitnesses and servants of the gospel'.[4] So clearly the writers are making use of older material. Some of this material, indeed, was evidently in Aramaic, the local language, and scraps of speech in Aramaic are occasionally quoted in the Greek text. On occasion it's as if the fingerprints of these eyewitnesses are right there on the evidence.

Apart from the Bible we also have other references to Jesus from major Roman historians. Tacitus, Suetonius and Pliny all mention him briefly, admittedly in all cases looking back at him because of an interest in the growing phenomenon of Christianity in their own time. A slightly fuller treatment is given in the writings of Josephus, a Jewish Roman closer to Jesus in time who is no particular friend of his and mentions him very much in passing, which oddly enough adds to its plausibility. In fact it is often incidental, seemingly unimportant historical references which are the most convincing. For example, Josephus himself reports that a certain James, 'brother of Jesus who is called Christ' was condemned in 62 CE to stoning for transgressing the Jewish Law. The reference has no real interest in Jesus as such, merely using him to identify his brother, and adding the 'who is called Christ' to distinguish him from all the other Jesuses who shared what was after all a fairly common name. The date at 62 CE is about right, and this James is presumably the brother of the same name who is mentioned in the Acts of the Apostles as the leader of the Christian community in Jerusalem. Then again the fourth-century Eusebius relates an account from the second-century Hegesippus that the emperor Domitian in the late first century CE had arrested and cross-examined the grandsons of Judas (one of Jesus' brothers, not the more notorious disciple), but then released them. Again this brother Judas is mentioned on one occasion in one of the Gospel narratives.

This level of evidence is never conclusive but often because of its very accidental nature it is the more convincing. So it turns out that the evidence for Jesus' existence is on balance not that bad, much better than for many historical figures whose existence we unhesitatingly accept.

However, since the late eighteenth century there have been authors making the case that the evidence for Jesus' existence is unconvincing, and that the figure of Jesus is more likely to have been a mythical invention of the times. To add legend in order to 'sex up' an already existing factual base is one thing, but inventing it from nothing is quite another proposition. Nevertheless, modern skeptics on this point are echoing themes already raised in the second century by writers like Trypho and Celsus, who likewise doubted whether Jesus had ever existed. Admittedly, both these writers – one Jewish, the other pagan – were writing consciously anti-Christian polemics, and for some this might weaken their case.

During the nineteenth century the argument that Jesus had not existed tended to overlap with arguments that much of the text of the Bible was unreliable in different ways, arguments which have influenced biblical experts today, and this book reflects some of this. The other argument with which it has become confused is that although a teacher called Jesus may have existed, the biblical and later Christian picture of him owes a great deal to legend formation and the attribution to him of a range of roles and sayings which were not his. Again this issue is taken seriously today, and it features throughout this book. Important elements in Jesus' teachings do reflect some of the themes of his times. He has some similarities, for example, with other groups like the Pharisees, the Essenes (of Dead Sea Scrolls fame), or other individuals like Hanina ben Dosa, who, like Jesus, addressed God in strikingly intimate terms. It is therefore easy to see him as summing up various currents of his time, or even as a conflation of them. There may indeed be a few grains of truth in all this, but in the end these arguments have to be weighed against other evidence.

In the case of Jesus it's the internal evidence that is probably most convincing, even despite the evident bias of the writing and its distance from him in time. Apart from anything else, had others invented this story from nothing they would surely have placed their hero in Judea. Indeed one of the four narratives does attempt to place at least his birth in Judea, but the mass of stories about Jesus are located in the province of Galilee of all places.

Galilee was historically a mongrel province, half Jewish and half pagan; in fact it was regarded as a bit of a joke by Judeans. For anyone interested in restoring the fortunes of the kingdom of Israel, Galilee is the last place they would have thought of looking to find their future leader. This repeated reference to Galilee does look like an eloquent unconscious witness to something authentic: a real historical figure behind the text.

The teaching itself, moreover, does seem to bear the hallmarks of a sharp intellect, reflecting some of the currents of the time but giving to them the stamp of one man's very personal insight. Besides, the four biblical narratives convey telling details of the way this individual related to people, and even the patterns and rhythms of his own way of speaking and thinking. The next few chapters will include some examples of these details. In these four accounts, then, it does seem that we are encountering some reasonably authentic detail mixed with distant memory, axe-grinding and legend formation, and sometimes it's hard to tell which is which. Yet underneath the other layers there is tantalizing evidence of a distinctive, highly individual person, evidence which doesn't sound as if someone else has made it up.

Archaeological discovery in the twentieth century has dramatically extended our knowledge of the many other writings of the historical period not long after the four New Testament Gospels were written, writings which originally circulated alongside them. These writings included further Gospels, epistles and other works, apparently dating mainly from the early second century. This book nevertheless will focus attention on the four narrative accounts in the Bible itself, because as far as we can see at present they are on the whole earlier, closer to the source, and contain less legend and more authentic material than most of the others. Study of these other writings continues; expert opinion is not unanimous and the consensus may yet change. For the present, however, although these other writings have enriched our understanding of early Christianity two generations and more after

Jesus, they seem less likely to add greatly to an authentic picture of Jesus in his own time. (There are one or two important exceptions to this view, and these will be mentioned later.)

Sifting the Evidence

The attempt to get back to an understanding of the original teachings of Jesus has been going on since at least the eighteenth century and continues today, enjoying a revival, as it happens, in the last two or three decades. (For a more detailed account of this whole field, see David Boulton, *Who on Earth was Jesus? The Modern Quest for the Jesus of History*.) In fact this modern quest picks up and continues, after a long gap, a lively debate about these very same questions in the first few centuries after Jesus.

In modern times Thomas Jefferson, one of the first presidents of the United States, was an early contributor to this renewed quest. Then at the turn of the twentieth century Albert Schweitzer published his magisterial *Quest of the Historical Jesus*, reviewing the modern quest up to his own time and seeing Jesus fundamentally as an apocalyptic prophet of the end of time. Schweitzer also posed the dilemma that a truly historical Jesus was likely to be largely irrelevant to people's needs today, whereas a relevant Jesus would turn out to be almost certainly unhistorical. This view does seem convincing at first sight but later work has questioned it as, in the end, too simple. Crucially, Jesus' teaching was evidently a good deal subtler than Schweitzer's understanding of it, something capable of coming to life in the hearts of people in very different historical times.

Following this line of reasoning, this book will investigate whether there are important elements in Jesus' teaching which are historically authentic in his own time and yet also have important things to say to people in our own time. Indeed it will argue that much of what has become inauthentic about modern images of Jesus derives from the distortions of later church doctrines in intervening centuries.

After Schweitzer, people lost interest for a time in the quest for a historical Jesus, but this then revived in the later twentieth century. For example, in recent decades the Jewish and Christian writer Geza Vermes, perhaps best known for his work on the Dead Sea Scrolls, has demonstrated through numerous telling details the typical Jewishness of Jesus in his own time.[5] To take just one example, the phrase 'son of man', a phrase frequently used by Jesus, was commonly used in the Aramaic of the time as a more indirect alternative to 'I', where the use of the first person pronoun might have seemed inappropriate, too direct, perhaps too boastful. Keith Akers, among others, has described the world of the early Jewish Christians, a group which features in Luke's Acts of the Apostles, who saw Jesus as the great second Moses, come to finish his work, to simplify and complete the Law.[6] The long speech of Stephen before his martyrdom, recorded at length in Luke's Acts of the Apostles, gives a flavor of this early Jewish Christianity.[7]

In the 1990s a group of biblical scholars in the United States calling themselves the Jesus Seminar undertook the task of systematically examining every verse containing sayings of Jesus in the four New Testament Gospels and also in the Sayings Gospel of Thomas.[8] They then classified each saying, by majority consensus, as either very likely to be authentic; in harmony with other authentic sayings but unlikely to be authentic in itself; on balance unlikely to be authentic; or definitely apocryphal, carefully detailing the reasons for and against in each case. Then in the later 1990s the Seminar attempted a similar evaluation of the reports of the deeds attributed to Jesus in the Gospel narratives. The work of the Jesus Seminar was almost bound to raise a storm of protest since it seemed to many people to shake the foundations of their beliefs. Others, however, sensed that it can sharpen and deepen our understanding. Such is the open quest for truth.

Other work has built a clearer picture of the various stages by which the life and teachings of Jesus were put on record. Already during the time of Jesus' teaching, the tradition of oral memorization and formal recitation, typical of so many societies before widespread literacy, had probably preserved a fairly close record of much of the central teaching and some of the events in his life. (This process is actually described in an apocryphal writing dated to the early second century, the Secret Book of James.) These oral records, some of them quite possibly origi- nating during Jesus' own time of teaching, would then no doubt quickly acquire a natural authority. At some point some of these were set down in writing and then eventually collected together in the first extended written collections of the sayings of Jesus, so-called Sayings Gospels.[9] One example of this genre is the Gospel of Thomas, rediscovered in its full text only in the twentieth century.

Then, in the late first century, somewhere between 35 and 70 years after the death of Jesus, the first narrative Gospels were assembled, written down, and over a period of time perhaps expanded and edited. Written against a setting, by this time, of still very small and often threatened early Christian communities spreading out from Palestine across the Roman world, it seems they were written in part to comfort these communities in times of periodic local persecution and also to establish a base of authority amid the by now competing versions of the story, as the oral tradition finally began to fragment and diversify.

Here too the tell-tale fingerprints of the period of writing are evident in the texts. For example, by this time Christians and Jews were rivals in faith, but often confused and lumped together in the minds of the pagan majority; hence perhaps the anti-Jewish flavor in parts of the narrative Gospels, especially in John's account, and the impression that Jesus was struggling against 'the Jews', as though he wasn't one of them himself! But perhaps above all, these four narratives depict in vivid detail the full remembered humanity of Jesus, encoding this in a series of acts which convey a definite symbolic meaning. In these Jesus heals, feeds, liberates, makes people see, walk, be whole again – all crucial symbolic elements in the story.

The first three narrative Gospels, probably first written between 65 and 85 CE, are often seen together because they use common material, both Matthew and Luke making extensive use of material already in Mark, which appears to have been written first. Matthew and Luke also seem to use material from another common source which Mark evidently didn't know, and which itself has been lost, usually referred to as Q, as well as material unique to each of them. ('Q' is for *Quelle*, coined first by German researchers. *Quelle* means 'source' in German.)

At the same time these three accounts are quite different from each other, written as they are in dramatically contrasting circumstances. Mark's account was quite possibly written in Rome itself and is full of action and urgency, showing Jesus as a mysterious, challenging figure, perhaps appealing to a wider readership in this pagan city. (In announcing it right at the start as 'the gospel [*evangelion*] of Jesus Christ the Son of God', Mark is provocatively imitating the style of the periodic *evangelia* issued by the emperors, the living gods who gave peace and prosperity to their peoples.[10]) Matthew, however, is writing in a more provincial setting apparently for a mainly Jewish Christian community, perhaps in Syria, and portrays a teacher in a Jewish prophetic tradition. Luke's account, by contrast, is probably written in Greece or Asia Minor for a Greek audience, and portrays Jesus as a just man who is concerned for suffering humanity.

The Gospel of John, written quite possibly in the great city of Ephesus, inhabits another world with a different take on Jesus: a deeply considered theological meditation on the meaning he had for its author. For some people John's account reads like a drama, written in a familiar Greek format for Greek readers, in which the central character is nothing less than the cosmic wisdom of God born in the human spirit. Still, although it was finished perhaps as much as 60 to 70 years after the events it describes, some experts believe that it contains quite a bit of material, for example geographical detail, personally remembered from Jesus' time.

Each of the four Gospels has its own take on the events it describes; indeed the accounts contradict each other at numerous points, and early readers presumably understood this. Although Matthew and Luke make use of material in Mark, they don't hesitate to change the wording or the context in which they place it, according to how they themselves understand its significance. For example, Matthew takes the hard-line remarks of Jesus on divorce as reported by Mark and significantly softens them for his own largely Jewish audience, for whom divorce was allowed. It seems that Matthew didn't agree with Mark at this point. There is an unconscious candor in this.

The four accounts repeatedly tell us that 'all this happened in order to make what the Lord had said through the prophet come true'. The writers were steeped in a tradition of prophecy, of a sense that historical events were building up to some fulfillment in the future, dimly discerned by seers in the past. If you believe this then you will tend to see events through this glass, and you will select those events which seem to fulfill this tradition of prophecy. Indeed the narrative itself as it is handed down will tend to acquire stories and details of, at times, dubious accuracy or even pure invention, included in perfect sincerity because they fit this overall view of things. The infancy stories in Matthew's account contain good examples of this. Jesus is born in Bethlehem, for example, and later Joseph takes the family into Egypt, all to fulfill some past prophecy.

Nevertheless, some experts have pointed out that the form of the narrative Gospel, in which a hero is unjustly persecuted and subsequently vindicated, is essentially Greek in origin. Some commentators have even seen quite a few similarities in characterization and storylines between the narrative of Mark and Luke – two writers who were evidently influenced by Greek culture – and the two great epic poems of Homer: the Iliad and the Odyssey.[11] These long sagas pervaded Greek culture. They were taught to children, performed in public readings, illustrated on vases and mosaics throughout the Greek-speaking world and among educated Romans. Like Homer's heroes, Jesus drives out demons, travels with foolish companions, conceals his true identity, makes a picaresque entry into a city, is anointed by a woman who recognizes who he really is, and predicts his own return. In writing their accounts, Mark and Luke quite naturally model them on the existing heroic narratives of their time.

At the same time, each Gospel is a considered statement, put together no doubt after much reflection, and each expressing a distilled consensus about the meaning of Jesus to its authors and its community. With the passage of time, while much of the detailed factual memory is bound to fade, the deeper meaning may actually become clearer. Gradually as time passed, those who had known Jesus as a friend died one by one and his compelling memory began to fade. Meanwhile other influences like Gnosticism were just starting to gain ground (see Chapter 14 for more on this), so the aim of the four narrative Gospels was also to assert their own memory and understanding of Jesus as against that of others.

Behind the four narrative Gospels, then, experts have revealed a picture of continuity and changing times, new trends of thought and conservative reactions. After all, it does appear that the ministry of Jesus had lasted a remarkably short time – some sources reckon between one and three years, others less than a year – and much of it came in the form of stories apparently challenging listeners to find their own response. This and the perhaps unexpected circumstances of his death left a legacy which must have been wide open to all kinds of interpretations in later times. For example, the idea that Jesus had died 'for our sins', undergoing a due punishment in our place, was one such early interpretation. The assertion three centuries later that he was 'of one substance with God the Father' was another.

So the Jesus which this book portrays is essentially the Jesus of the four Gospels, that is, a conflation of four quite distinct accounts set down in the late first century. Expert opinion has drawn our attention to the human distortion, bias and in places sheer invention of these four narratives, but also draws attention to a considerable mass of apparently authentic detail in the text, detail which appears to reveal an unmistakable human being. These four accounts are a mix of both elements – legend *and* memory – and although the memory is distant, it does seem to have been based on a carefully memorized and frequently recited oral tradition which appears to derive from an earlier period a good deal closer to the original. (Two modern authors have recently called for a new appreciation of this portrait of Jesus embedded within the text of the four biblical accounts. [12])

Some of the expert analysis available today distinguishes within the text of the four narratives some material which is considered to be earlier than the rest and which gives a distinctive, perhaps particularly early picture of Jesus. The material unique to Matthew and Luke and the material from the source Q common to both accounts is picked out for special attention. This early picture is then apparently corroborated by material in other, non-canonical writing of the time, particularly the Didache, the Gospel of Philip and the already mentioned Gospel of Thomas. These are also thought by some to date from an early period, perhaps as early as 50 CE, that is, possibly a couple of decades before the four narrative Gospels were assembled and written. This book, however, retains a touch of skepticism on all this. These findings are, in the end, provisional and dependent among other things on the chance of archaeological good fortune. Who knows what may yet be unearthed from the sands of Egypt or Palestine?

Besides, the commendable caution with which many experts proceed may ironically have honed down the picture of Jesus too far, producing an over-rationalized Jesus, an over-analyzed minimalist picture as seen by twentieth and twenty-first century minds. In the end the Jesus who made such a profound impression on those who heard him was probably more than just a wisdom teacher. People don't crucify a wisdom teacher. He was evidently altogether more passionate, more colorful and more challenging than this, apparently playing a shadowy, ambiguous, easily misunderstood role in his own politically explosive times.

Also, the evident brevity of his period of inspiration, and the depth of the learning process he went through in that short time, may indicate a point of view and a teaching which may still have contained some unresolved contradictions. Indeed this would be very characteristic of the heat of a visionary's inspiration in such times, and we do get a definite feel of this from the narratives. So modern experts, constrained by the necessary limits of their own logic, may have succeeded in producing only a partial, perhaps over-intellectualized portrait. The reality may have been altogether less tidy, and a good deal more passionate and more challenging.

Cultural Distance

In trying to understand Jesus for our own time, we need to be clear that our understanding is going to be limited in the same way, constrained by the limits of our twenty-first century minds. It's as if we are trying to picture him using a twenty-first century mirror, with its own distortions and blind areas. Perhaps that is the best we can do. On the one hand we must try hard to avoid shoehorning him into the picture we want to see. On the other hand the whole point of this is to see in what ways it speaks to our needs today. So the next few chapters, I think quite legitimately, will have to be partly about us in our day, as well as about Jesus in his day.

The past, it has been said, is a foreign country. On the one hand we often have enticing scraps of incidental detail, for example about spoken accents – Jesus presumably spoke with the same thick Galilean accent which got Peter into such hot water just after the arrest, as the cocks crew and the city awoke to another day. On the other hand historical evidence is always going to be limited. More fundamentally, the attempt to get inside the mindset of another period of history can be bafflingly difficult.

For example, in the text of the narrative Gospels Jesus is shown traveling through the countryside in the company of a group of followers, and therefore some people assume that he is unmarried. This issue is of some importance since it may have exerted influence on later traditions extolling celibacy. Others point out that this traveling ministry was evidently only for a relatively short time. Some have even argued that Jesus must have been married, because marriage was so universal in that society that if he had not been married it would have attracted immediate comment. However, Paul in a single reference in one of his letters seems to indicate, very much in passing, that Jesus was not married.[13]

In a similar vein there has been speculation in modern times that Jesus may have been gay.[14] Reference is often made to the disciple whom Jesus loved, and even to a young man dressed only in a linen cloth who mysteriously turns up in the story of Jesus' arrest. The most we can say surely is that this level of evidence is much too sketchy to permit us to draw any definite conclusions. Indeed the very question perhaps reflects our own sex-obsessed and curiously bone-headed, literal-minded times. It's clear that Jesus was evidently not your standard stereotypical male – thank God for that, some might add – but to go beyond that would be simply to indulge in speculation and perhaps wishful thinking.

It really goes without saying that a part of Jesus will probably remain culturally quite strange to our eyes. He isn't going to be like the chap next door. For example, he seems to have been a healer in a tradition recognized within his own culture. On one occasion, the narrative records, he spat on the ground, made a paste of soil and saliva, and applied this to a blind man's eyes, telling him to wash it off in the pool of Siloam, a well which served as a reservoir for the city and was widely thought to have healing properties.[15] It does seem pretty unlikely that Jesus was making up this elaborate routine as he went along. He treated different cases in different ways. This looks like a procedure learned as part of a tradition of folk healing, one of a range of responses open to him depending on closely observing individual symptoms.

One author argues that an early strand of symbolic thought linked Jesus with the Jerusalem temple and its liturgy, a whole world which would soon be swept away quite literally by the Roman military.[16] This tradition of thought also apparently saw his mother Mary as an incarnation of the Holy Wisdom, which in some Jewish thinking was often given a female face. This strand of Jewish Christian logic is fascinating and not implausible for the time, a time which was evidently alive with many strands of thinking claiming to interpret this enigmatic new teacher.

Jesus also seems to have believed that history at some point in the future would be rolled up like a map, and some of his followers believed that he would be the agent used by God to right wrongs and wipe away all tears. Other experts believe this was more about the end of the Roman Empire rather than the end of time itself, but Jesus does seem to have expected some kind of heavenly intervention, perhaps after a period of chaos and suffering. Perhaps this is one reason why no one thought it necessary to write an account of Jesus until a whole generation later – people believed that he would come back very soon in any case.

Clearly, some of the ideas which preoccupied Jesus in his own time mean very little to us today. In one of them, the idea of a divine intervention in the clouds, he does seem to have turned out to be mistaken: Jesus did not return in the way people seem to have expected. To say this may come as something of a shock, especially to people who have been taught that Jesus was in some way incapable of making mistakes. Yet there may be more to this. The twin themes of healing the human condition and of a Kingdom within us all are at the very core of Jesus' teaching. Perhaps they can still speak to us symbolically today, even though we can no longer be part of his world-view in any literal sense.

Chapter 3
A Figure Comes into Focus

Logic in the Evidence

The four narrative Gospels express late first-century understandings of Jesus; that is, their point of view reflects a very
particular juncture in history. They are written far from
Palestine, mainly after the destruction of the Jerusalem temple in
70 CE, an event of enormous importance to early followers,
many of whom would be dispersed far and wide into a largely
Greek pagan world. As we saw in the previous chapter, the
writers make use of oral memory from the earlier time of Jesus'
teaching, but they interpret it with the language and assumptions of utterly different times, times in which their whole world
has been turned upside down.

This is why it is possible, after all, for experts to attempt to
tease apart authentic sayings of Jesus from these later points of
view, frequently right there in the next verse. Of course there will
always be some degree of uncertainty and disagreement about
the details of this, verse by verse. On balance, however, the
differences right there in the text do create a basis permitting us
today to focus more precisely on the authority of Jesus' own
teaching, as distinct from the words of his interpreters. This
means that we can see its major themes more clearly and we can
pay more attention to what is distinctive about them. By any
standards this is surely a development of the first rank of importance, already influencing how many Christians understand
their faith.

Some commentators have taken the view that the New
Testament scripture is irreducibly the view of a later generation,
and that the work of separating out an authentic pre-crucifixion
teaching is in the end just too uncertain. For example, when Luke

describes Jesus' concern for the underprivileged and for those who suffer, does this reflect the values of Jesus or those of the narrator's own educated Greek world? Luke's Gospel does depict Jesus as the ideal model of humanity, an important idea within Greek culture. Presumably it reflects both situations to some extent, but it seems implausible that Luke had largely invented these ideas and that they reflect largely his own Greek world. There is a substratum, a reality which has moved Luke to write in the first place, and while being thoroughly Greek, he is also well versed in the world of Jewish belief and experience.[17] In the end this pessimistic view that all we have are the words of the followers seems willfully to be turning its back on important strands of logic within the evidence, strands which do come together to form a distinctive picture.

Thanks to the painstaking work of many scholars over a long period of time, today we do have a more adequate basis for piecing together the picture of one man's distinctive teaching. This has its own internal coherence and startling vision, its own key themes and distinctive leitmotivs, couched in its own Aramaic language and expressing its own very Jewish world and aspirations. Despite differences between experts, it does seem that a clearer outline of the main themes of this teaching can now be made. We can now see it more clearly as the foundation on which a whole series of later elaborations were then built.

The importance of this is that it can give us a foundation on which we too can proceed. Since we can now distinguish the main outlines of Jesus' own teaching with a new degree of clarity, later doctrines can be revisited and seen in the light of it. These doctrines may of course agree with this teaching or indeed enhance it, but in places where a doctrine seems to undermine it or to replace it with something else which distracts our attention away from it, we can now quite reasonably pencil in a question mark against any such doctrine, can we not?

What we're doing, moreover, is within a long tradition of

intelligent re-understanding and reformulation of the original vision, going right back to the start in fact. After Jesus' death his followers meditated on the remembered teachings and in time came to a new understanding. Some time after this, Paul, Luke, John and others had the problem of translating this into the mindset of non-Jewish, Greek-speaking polytheists, and a further new understanding arose. In one way or another there have been people doing this kind of thing ever since, in every age, bringing fresh words to the original vision, allowing it to speak to people in their own time.

Today it's clear that some important things in our picture of Jesus are badly wrong. This man who was made into the ultimate establishment figure of all time was in reality shockingly disreputable. Possibly conceived out of wedlock, he left home, wandering the countryside in the company of a group of young men. He not only spoke to down-and-outs but sought out their company and ate and drank with them. And this is the savior of the earth? To even hint at this can be shocking to some people today, but much of this detail in the narrative appears to be deliberate. It does seem that the authors intended to create a real memory of Jesus, possibly correcting a growing tendency at the time to see him as a largely unreal cosmic figure.

Even more peculiar, for most of these later centuries many of Jesus' teachings have been subtly sidelined, moved out from the central core, the test of Christian belief. Of course the teachings were preserved in the text of what later became the sacred canon of the faith, the New Testament, and people in all centuries have been inspired by them. Nevertheless the meaning of the teachings has been to an extent blurred and their impact diluted by the attention paid to later doctrines and disputes. The great creeds of the late classical period barely even mention them. But the teachings are crucial. Are they not the spring from which everything else flowed?

The Sound of Laughter

There are other forgotten sides to this man's personality which can come as quite a surprise to us in modern times, revealed to us especially in some scraps of detail in the accounts of Matthew and Luke.[18] Here is someone whose way of talking to people easily turns to banter or teasing, who has a taste for vivid word-pictures, exaggeration and the absurd, who is not above a bit of clowning, and who appears to have a talent to make people smile.

Here he is commenting on the reception people gave to John the Baptist and then to himself, revealing a very individual way of saying things.

How can I describe the people of this generation? What are they like? They are like children sitting in the marketplace and calling to each other,

We piped for you and you would not dance.

We lamented, and you would not mourn.

For John the Baptist came, neither eating bread nor drinking wine, and you say, 'He is possessed.' The Son of Man came, eating and drinking, and you say, 'Look at him! A glutton and a drinker, a friend of tax-collectors and sinners!'[19]

It's not hard to imagine the long, mocking face or even a falsetto voice as he imitates first the kids playing in the street and then his po-faced critics! Just a few verses before this, Luke's account shows him quizzing the crowd: 'What did you go out into the wilderness to see? A reed swaying in the wind? No? Then what did you go out to see? A man dressed in finery? Grand clothes and luxury are to be found in palaces.' Can you catch the twinkle in the eyes accompanying this good-natured leg-pulling? Notice that the narrator has thought this detail worth including in his Gospel. It evidently mattered to him.

Here is Jesus again, this time indoors at a dinner in the house of a Pharisee replying to implied criticism that he has just infringed the Sabbath laws by healing a man: 'If one of you has a donkey or an ox that falls into a well, will he hesitate to pull him out on the sabbath day?'[20] Other people might have replied in a more sober fashion, but this man just couldn't resist painting this word-picture, as graphic as a comic strip. It's easy to imagine the scene as the smiles go round the table. Jesus is answering the criticism by using humor to defuse it and at the same time to charm his audience! And here is what he says to his followers about the same Pharisees, the great foils for Jesus set up by the narrators of the Gospels: 'Leave them alone; they are blind guides, and if one blind man guides another they will both fall into the ditch.'[21] Again what we get is a word-picture, and again an edge of dry humor which seems to come naturally to him. Jewish humor was apparently alive and well 2,000 years ago!

This is Jesus famously commenting on wealth, perhaps in reply to a question from a follower or from the crowd: 'How hard it is for the wealthy to enter the kingdom of God! It is easier for a camel to go through the eye of a needle than for a rich man to enter the kingdom of God.'[22] Was he using a well-known folk saying, a turn of phrase in common use in the Aramaic of the time, or was this phrase his own invention? It's such a strange image that some have wondered whether the Eye of the Needle was perhaps the name of a very narrow gate in the city walls of Jerusalem. This would seem to fit, but sadly there is no evidence confirming this ingenious explanation in any other source. Either way, here we are with another graphic word-sketch. Camels are comical beasts, as Jesus and his hearers well knew. Perhaps you can hear the guffaws from the back of the crowd.

Again here he is advising people on how *not* to help others, again irresistibly drawn to graphic exaggeration: 'When you give alms, do not announce it with a flourish of trumpets, as the hypocrites do in synagogues and in the streets to win the praise of others.'[23] In contrast, here he is encouraging his followers in private, chiding them more gently for being too timorous: 'You are light for all the world ... When a lamp is lit, it is not put under the meal-tub, but on the lampstand, where it gives light to everyone in the house.'[24] With gentle skill he persuades his friends by first making them smile.

Does this resemble the stern, unsmiling Jesus we thought we knew? Here in the Gospel record we are given just a few extraordinary glimpses of this man in the street and in people's homes, making people laugh and think twice at the same time. He is perfectly comfortable getting a laugh even with lavatory humor! Here he comments on Jewish dietary laws: 'Do you not see that nothing that goes into a person from outside can defile him, because it does not go into the heart but into the stomach, and so goes out into the drain?'[25] He didn't need that last phrase, but perhaps he just couldn't resist it! Could anyone have invented a character with this very particular, sharp-eyed, comical way of looking at things? It's possible, but it's surely more likely that we are catching a glimpse of a very particular individual with his own way of talking to people, challenging them, teasing them and making them smile with his droll observations of life.

He can be quick-witted on his feet, too. Someone throws him a highly political question: 'Are we or are we not permitted to pay taxes to the Roman emperor?' This is happening within the Jerusalem temple complex, in public, and if he says either yes or no he could land himself in trouble.

> 'Show me the coin used for the tax.' They handed him a silver piece. Jesus asked, 'Whose head is this, and whose inscription?' 'Caesar's,' they replied.
> He said to them, 'Then pay to Caesar what belongs to Caesar, and to God what belongs to God.'[26]

Perhaps it's the quick, wide-eyed innocence of the reply that causes the bystanders to smile. You can almost catch him winking at the crowd! The idea that just because Caesar's face is on the coin it must logically belong to Caesar may at first sight appear to be like a child's point of view, but it has, on reflection, an edge of mockery to it. The Romans and their friends certainly did get the lion's share of any money that was going, so in a funny way it *is* quite logical that their emperor's face should appear on the coins! The Hebrew scriptures, by contrast, were very clear that the earth is the Lord's and belongs to no man.

The man we are meeting here is evidently a strong character, someone people remember and are drawn to because of his larger-than-life energy, his compassion with the downtrodden, his anger at the hypocrites, his memorable skill at telling a good story, and his growing fame as a healer, touching the untouchables, and through all this his flashing, dry humor.

And it's not hard to understand the affection with which the writers of the Gospels remembered their teacher as they related these incidents all these years later, incidents which people had no doubt told and retold down the years. Clearly Jesus' wit, his very turns of phrase and his way of making people smile were remembered and treasured, important enough to tell again when they came to write their record of him and what he meant to them.

The Woman who Caressed His Feet

In our quest the outline of one unmistakable human being is beginning to emerge. One more glimpse, this time in its way quite dramatic, of how people responded to him, and how he responded to them in return. Again superficially this is quite a well-known story. Jesus is a guest at table in the house of (yet another) Pharisee. Evidently he is becoming quite a celebrity locally.

A woman who was living an immoral life in the town had learned that Jesus was a guest in the Pharisee's house and had brought oil of myrrh in a small flask. She took her place behind him, by his feet, weeping. His feet were wet with her tears and she wiped them with her hair, kissing them and anointing them with the myrrh.[27]

How sensational, how moving and yet how full of emotional ambiguity this scene is. Who can guess what drove this woman to her present state, and exactly what it is she is letting out in her tears? What mixture of anger, guilt or mourning burdens her?

Perhaps most striking of all is the sexual charge in the encounter. This experienced woman doesn't just touch his feet maybe once or twice; she kisses them and caresses them continuously with her hands and her hair! This is presumably in front of a number of other men and possibly some serving women as well. What are they all thinking?! Jesus says at one point that she has been kissing his feet ever since he came in! Not content with this, she then massages them with the myrrh oil. Even her gift is highly sensual, expressing herself and her world, and for those who are so minded it's not difficult to read a further invitation behind this generosity!

Actually to touch Jesus, for a low-status, unclean woman in this situation is more than just a bit cheeky. It's not just that she is potentially compromising him in this intimate way in a public situation. What she is doing is outrageous because in the eyes of Jewish custom of the time she is polluting him. This woman is allegedly notorious, perhaps in effect a prostitute, and this makes her behavior especially provocative, and she surely knows this. Jesus is a man in his early thirties. What does he do?

He doesn't pull back in horror or disapproval, and he doesn't try to stop her. Not once does he question her motives or her character. He accepts what she does, allows her to cry herself out and waits until she is finished. This in itself is quite something! He is probably surprised and perhaps in some degree attracted, very much in the way we would expect a man of his age to be. He is also quite possibly moved. The only lesson worth drawing, he says later, goes something like this: the greater a person's grief or their need to be forgiven, the greater will be their gratitude and love. Sincere grief and sorrow like this generates from the creator an instant and generous compassion, every time, quite naturally, quite regardless of the offense or the reputation of the person concerned.

Jesus is often remembered for his words. This occasion, however, is one in which he says very little, simply letting his actions speak, evidently part of a distinctive personal style. Did he look directly at her, or did he look discreetly away? The blessing might have surprised her, spoken perhaps in a half-whisper, and a firm hint sending her on her way: 'All your sins are forgiven. Your own faith has saved you. Go in peace.'

Our understanding of the force of Jesus' teaching has faded perhaps because we have lost any real sense of his humanity in the round. Fortunately the evidence of this humanity is here preserved in all its drama in this scrap of narrative record.

Reader Beware!

I suspect we will have to keep reminding ourselves again and again to set aside the great panoply of ideas that later history has attached to him: Jesus as the stern power above the political establishments of the world, or as the god-figure play-acting the role of a man. We may then catch a glimpse of the wandering teacher who related instinctively to the outcasts, who saw a new vision of what all humanity could become, at peace with itself and its maker.

In writing about this new vision, the first three of the narrative Gospels use the terms 'Kingdom of God' and 'Kingdom of Heaven' more or less interchangeably, the latter term being perhaps more Jewish, reflecting a hesitancy to talk of the mystery of God directly. In this book I also use the latter term because of an oddly similar hesitancy in our own culture and time. Many people today find it unhelpful to use the word 'God' because for them it is still associated with a hostile or even vengeful image. Others again find it hard to believe in a quasi-human personality behind our infinite and mysterious creation. I have some sympathy with both of these views. Yet it is not really possible to talk about Jesus in his own time without using the word 'God', since it was so full of meaning for him. (See Chapter 16 for more on this theme.) It would be unbearably artificial to constantly skate round the word – more straightforward by far to simply use it broadly as he understood it, as far as we can see.

What was this Kingdom of Heaven about? It wasn't about a political kingdom on earth, although the origins of the idea were profoundly political and some early Christian followers evidently still saw it that way. Nor was it about a kingdom in the sky with its own cosmological coordinates. Wherever else this new Kingdom existed, it existed within the human heart, as a whole new inner dimension which can transform how we see ourselves.

Nevertheless, just before we start, perhaps there should also be some kind of caveat to the reader. Jesus holds up a mirror to us, and what we see may not be exactly comfortable. He shows us how he sees us and he does this with an uncompromising honesty which may not be to everyone's taste. This teaching can stir our emotions and can be personally challenging. Let the reader beware!

Part Two
A New Inner Landscape

Part Two of this book explores and sets out Jesus' extraordinary teaching about a Kingdom of Heaven which is within each of us and yet is also among us. It examines where it may have come from and the stages it may have gone through, and it follows the logic of this teaching through a whole series of interconnected topics. It finds a coherence and depth in this teaching, but it also ponders the strangeness of its enigmatic challenge and appeal.

In the process of doing this, Part Two also draws several more sketches of Jesus and one fuller portrait, picking out points of human detail and tracing strands of logic within the four biblical narratives. Finally it assesses the scale of this man's achievement, seen against the culture of his own time and also against the wider backdrop of human history.

Chapter 4
The Mind of a Storyteller

Teaching and Saving

People today think of Jesus as either a savior or a teacher, and although for some there is a natural connection between these two roles, for others this connection is more problematic. One problem is that whereas the role of savior is usually stated in clear, often formulaic words, the role of teacher is much more vaguely understood and remembered. It's as if lip service is being paid to the teaching, but what really matters is the saving. Marcus Borg puts the traditional definition of the savior role like this:

> Who was he? The divinely begotten Son of God. What was his mission or purpose? To die for the sins of the world. What was his message? Most centrally, it was about himself: his own identity as the Son of God, the saving purpose of his death, and the importance of believing in him.[28]

For many non-Christian people these words have simply no meaning. It's as if they are being asked to believe that a man called Jesus just happened to be the Son of God, that his death as it happens saves them from something, and that as it happens all they have to do is believe all this. This does look like another example of the effects of centuries of hindsight thinking and an over-reliance on authority. Something has been lost here; somehow we have to restore the connections. If there is any truth in the saving role, isn't it likely to lie in the truth of the teaching? This book assumes that there is indeed an intended logic linking the two, and it sets out to find it. This is why it starts with the teaching, and examines the savior role later, seeing it in the light of the teaching.

Another point follows from this. If your belief centers on the saving action of Jesus in the events of the passion story, then quite possibly the details of the human being and how he came by his teaching may be of less interest. In effect you may be content with a two-dimensional, largely theological figure. But if you start with the teachings then the whole question of making sense of Jesus as a human being is likely to be more central and more interesting.

Christianity started not with a calmly laid-out set of doctrines but with urgency, frequent misunderstanding, high drama and mystery. It was hard enough to make sense of this radically new and sometimes enigmatic teaching, but then on top of that his followers had to make sense of the confusing and distressing events which happened at the end of his period of teaching. How were they supposed to arrive at one set of beliefs which tied all this together?

In fact they came up with all sorts of answers, none of which really made a final and unambiguous sense of it. It is hardly surprising that it took a long time – a few more centuries of debate and dissent, in fact – to sort out something like an orthodox point of view.

At first perhaps the events of the passion would have been interpreted quite naturally in the light of the teaching which had preceded them. Some time later, however, a kind of reverse logic may have begun to make itself felt, and soon the earlier teaching began to be reinterpreted in the light of the later turbulent events of the passion. Those who took the new faith to the surrounding pagan culture tended quite strongly to see things in this new way, perhaps because it made a natural sense to pagan minds of the time, apart from being an unforgettable drama.

A later Christianity has arguably held to this later view, although the earlier logic did survive, embedded in the new canon of scripture. This book re-examines this earlier logic, trying to reconfigure and re-understand the pre-crucifixion teaching on its own terms, and then see what light this might throw on the passion events. It does seem likely that many people right at the start would have done just this, and it is their logic that this book has now set out to retrace.

Seeing the World from the Inside Out

Jesus was teaching in a world which really had been turned upside down, as the savage requirements of Roman economic repression cynically reversed the logic of anything resembling a just community. The very hills cried out for justice, yet the overwhelming military strength of Roman power was unanswerable. After years of puzzling out this apparently insoluble conundrum, his eventual response was a remarkable leap of the imagination, reversing this reversal with his own logic in a teaching which took everyone by surprise. This was truly a logic not of this world, sidestepping yet getting under the defenses of all earthly power systems.

The gestation period for this extraordinary shift in understanding may have lasted quite a few years, but it seems clear from the four Gospel accounts that Jesus' resulting teaching period was really very short, so short indeed that many of his followers may have had only a partial understanding of what it meant. In fact this failure of understanding among his followers is reported on several occasions in the four accounts themselves. It may even be that as Jesus' vision deepened so dramatically within that short period of time, it became increasingly difficult for his followers to keep up with him. Peter, for example, saw him as the Messiah, the one anointed by God to free Israel, but at first he didn't understand what that would entail – how could he? In the end Jesus didn't free Israel at all, although he seemed to promise to do so.

In any case Jesus wasn't really a writer. The record shows a man who is first and foremost interested in meeting and interacting with people eye to eye, often in small groups in the open air. His skills are the skills of a public speaker, a crowd handler, using humor, anecdote and challenge, and his teaching is designed to provoke a response, to make the listener sit up and listen. This means that he has to get past ingrained habitual ways of thinking, not an easy task at the best of times. You can feel his frustration as he prefaces his sayings with 'Those with ears to hear, let them hear'. This frustration seems to be built into the situation he finds himself in. His teaching time and again seems quite deliberately to subvert the familiar world and to defy common sense. Again and again we read of people who struggle to understand him, like Nicodemus tying himself in knots over the idea of being born a second time, by any standards a startling idea to try to get across.[29] His way of thinking and his appeal to us seems to have the freewheeling logic of a poet or of a traditional storyteller rather than that of a philosopher.

How does Jesus speak of his own extraordinary vision? He tells stories about ordinary lives in a village setting. He speaks of crops and livestock, sheep and goats, vines and mustard bushes, sowing seeds, full harvests and famine, of farm owners, stewards and day laborers, of buying and selling and paying wages. When he invites us to follow him he uses a countryman's turn of phrase, a phrase which could have been spoken by a village carpenter, proud of his handiwork, inviting us to take his yoke upon us as if we are cattle drawing the plow, saying his yoke is easy and his burden light. He tells of the lilies of the field and the generous bounty of nature. He speaks of the shepherd knowing all his sheep by name and worrying more about his one sheep that has got itself lost rather than all the others safe in the fold. Only a countryman would use images like these and surely only someone from pastoral hill country would think of comparing humanity to sheep and goats! The language Jesus uses provides vivid snapshots of the world he knew intimately and grew up in, shaping the way he thought.

Perhaps it's in the sayings we know as the beatitudes that the logic of the everyday world is reversed and paradox is brought center stage most deliberately.[30] It is said that Gandhi once commented that this teaching was wonderful but it was such a pity that no one had actually tried to follow it, yet this is maybe because it was so difficult to understand what it was driving at. Here is a series of statements which on their own apparently make no sense, or only a shadowy kind of sense here and there. 'Blessed are the meek: for they shall inherit the earth.'(as translated in the Authorized Version) 'Oh yes, a likely story,' someone might reply. 'And if they ever did inherit the earth, they wouldn't be meek for very much longer!' These statements appear to be consciously paradoxical; they seem intended to provoke further thought in a classic tradition of the spiritual riddle which can be found in many cultures, both east and west.

This inner world which Jesus calls a Kingdom is evidently close to the surface world but is also a direct challenge to all its selfish, cynical, violent ways. Quite simply, it's about us and it can echo within us deep down if we take time to reflect on it. This is an original, not to say startling take on the world, seeing right through surface appearances. Little wonder that people at the time found it hard to grasp! Despite all appearances to the contrary, this inner Kingdom of trust, compassion and peace is closer to the heart's desire, and that is why in the end it will prevail.

Alongside this, at the very center of Jesus' teaching, is a teaching about how his God reigns in this inner world. Of course in Jesus' times the idea of God was a given – for almost everyone, atheism was simply inconceivable – but watch what he says about his God. He does use the word 'Kingdom', but this is no ordinary king, no distant giant ruling the universe from on high. This God is near, he says, right here among us, closer than breathing. More than that, he is alive, working dynamically within each of us, all the time, waking or sleeping. This is one reason why Jesus caused such a sensation around him in his own time, especially among the people at the bottom of the pile who had nothing else. The God Jesus saw is a profoundly intimate presence accompanying every one of us through all our lives, knowing us better than we know ourselves, intimately bound up with the affairs which preoccupy us day in, day out. Jesus calls him 'Abba'. This is usually translated as 'Father', but it might get closer to it to say 'Dad'. This might sound odd at first, but what we are trying to translate here is a close and tender form of address.

So much of Jesus' teaching quotes from the Hebrew Bible and takes its key words and ideas from Jewish tradition, yet it is startling in its originality. The Kingdom of Heaven, a cleansed Israel reconciled to its God and free of Roman occupation, is a familiar idea to those around him, but Jesus' understanding of it is distinctive and potent. Since Jesus' Kingdom is a presence within every human being, this means that we are never alone, so it allows us to keep hope alive in the worst of times. From a perfectly familiar Jewish idea, Jesus has created a whole landscape of new possibilities for ordinary people living ordinary lives everywhere.

How did Jesus arrive at such striking insight? Right from the start his family seem to have had high hopes of him. People today forget that Jesus was not his given name. Iesus is the Latin trans-lation of the Hebrew name Joshua, and the Greek translation is Iesous. In his mother tongue, Aramaic, a language related to Hebrew, he was called Yeshu, apparently a diminutive of Joshua. The name means 'savior', and was the name given in Jewish history to the leader who came after Moses and who led his people out of the desert, across the river Jordan into a promised land. So even the name his parents gave him contains an expected agenda, and a deeply Jewish one at that. When the writers of the four Gospels, writing in Greek for a Greek-speaking readership, then refer to him as Iesous, this has the effect of taking him out of the Jewish context in which he thought and lived, and portraying him as a world figure. There are indeed pros and cons to this – his teaching certainly had something to say to people across many cultures – but it does tend to airbrush out some of his essentially Jewish agenda and mindset.

In an age in which people believed in astrology and tried to interpret omens in order to foretell the future, it is perfectly plausible that a child born under very unusual circumstances, with dream visitations and all the rest, might be expected to become somebody special. Quite early, Jesus had learned his Jewish scripture, learning to interpret it freely and creatively (as Luke hints at in a story from his childhood[31]) meditating on the meaning underneath the surface, and in later years trying to work out how this might apply to the problems of his own times. Somewhere along the line, he may have spent some years learning the art of the folk-healer from a master in the traditional way. Practicing as a healer is then liable to bring you into contact with the full range of humanity, right down to the oppressed and the outcasts at the bottom of the heap.

At first it seemed that the Baptist's call to repentance summed up his own position pretty well. Then, as his vision deepened, it became clear that he needed to proclaim something much fuller, something which caught a sense of bringing exiled humanity home, and bringing their creator down and in among the people, among those very outcasts of society. Not long after, perhaps on hearing the shocking news of John's sudden arrest and capricious, casual murder, he changes course and apparently quite rapidly launches out on his own career as a teacher. It's as if he's more than ready for this, at last finally clear and confident about his own distinctive, rapidly deepening message, a message which would go altogether deeper than that of the kinsman from whom he had learned and whom he had now surpassed.

But this was going to be dangerous work. Some of the sense of urgency in the narrative record arises no doubt from the intensity and sheer speed with which his insight developed, but perhaps it also reflects his sense that he must press on with his proclamation quickly before the authorities put an end to it and to him. This began to seem like a race against time.

Inspiration for Jesus' stories had also no doubt arisen originally during his early years, observing ordinary people in everyday situations, seeing their yearnings remain unfulfilled amid a harsh reality. Conceived in controversial circumstances, is it possible that he knew from personal experience the public stigma of illegitimacy? Was he truly a man of sorrows, carrying an unspecified personal or family grief, and did this give a special edge to his understanding, related especially by Luke, for the little people at the edge of society?

The Wellspring: Abba

Of his parents, his mother Miriam (whom we know as Mary) seems to have been the creative thinker, something of a mystic in her own right, evidently a strong personality and a major influence on her son, in effect setting out his whole starting agenda. Luke has her prophesy at length about the God of Israel feeding the hungry with good things and sending the rich empty away. This is impassioned and yet paradoxical language, religiously perceptive and politically radical at one and the same time. Miriam, then, was a visionary, whereas her husband Joseph was, well, just a craftsman, and perhaps easy for us to overlook. After the infancy stories he is no longer mentioned, having probably died in the intervening years. He was no doubt older than his wife by quite a few years, possibly by a decade or two.

Yet Joseph's influence on his son fairly stares us in the face, when we think about it. Jesus' later, startlingly innovative experience of the God of Israel is of the warm, close and enveloping love of a presence he called Abba – the same intimate, tender name by which he had called his own father. Isn't this an enormous unconscious compliment to the man who had loved him and cradled him in his arms as a child? Isn't it possible that the growing awareness of this Abba within Jesus as a young adult may have been part of a complex delayed response to the earlier loss in tender years of a much-loved father?

The resulting vision of God, although recognizably within Jesus' own tradition, is arresting in the way it uses the intimate language of family life. This was new and it made people stop short. Put simply, this God sees you with the unreasoning enthusiasm of an adoring parent. Perhaps we too need to stop for a moment just to drink this in. This is where the slightly crazy, doting father in the prodigal son story comes from. The point about this God is that, like the best of parents, he actually thinks you're more wonderful than words can say. This once hit me like an electric jolt, changing the direction of my entire life, teaching me at long last to hold my head up and believe in myself. It also banished for ever the old frowning, vaguely disapproving sky god who still occasionally haunts the imagination of Christian people today. What is distinctive and unmistakable about the God of Jesus is his intimate and ebullient love for his creatures. If you had to sum up Jesus' whole teaching in one insight, perhaps this would have to be it.

This insight is so surprising, though, that at first it can feel like a double take. This can't possibly be right, we think; it must refer to somebody else far more deserving than I am. Somehow we can't quite bring ourselves to believe that we're really worth this kind of sublime response, and it takes time for it to really sink in. What if our entire surrounding reality, the reality which gave us birth, actually responds to us with an unfeigned delight and celebrates our beauty as spontaneously and as intensely as parents at their best would do with their own newborn child?!

This is not about cosmology; it's about a key which can unlock the human heart. It is also, of course, pure poetry and if we finally do respond to it we respond to it as poetry, but poetry which can let us glimpse a new picture of ourselves. For us today this insight can reveal to us in a flash the immense passion of the creation itself and the intimacy with which it expresses this passion within every one of us. Suddenly it can occur to us that up to now we have been in some way blind, alienated from ourselves and from our whole reality. The God seen by Jesus sets us back into that dazzling reality and reconciles us with it. We are loved more than we can know. The surprise and the drama of this can hit us like a tidal wave, yet it does begin to makes a certain very human sense. In the words of the Psalms, we have been given a new song.

What kind of man, then, was this father who was evidently the model for Jesus' central insight? Miriam could see the archangel. Her husband worked in wood, a man with strong roots (we might say) in the natural world. Yet Joseph could dream too, and it was his dreams which had given him the courage to commit himself to an uncertain future with this perhaps tempestuous woman. This in time led to the passionate, inspiring love of this ageing father for his amazing, beautiful child, and it was the child's later memory of that love that was destined to change history.

The teaching which in time emerged is recorded in the four Gospels in what appear to us to be fragments, apparently juxtaposed in order to convey a particular meaning, but a meaning to other people in other times, a good deal of which is lost to us today. Yet we can still piece together from this a teaching whose many insights do interlock. This is a single, internally coherent vision, a vision which hangs together, evidently the product of long gestation, and at its center is the entirely new reality of a Kingdom, an inner realm, within the human heart itself.

Chapter 5
Laying New Foundations

The Desert Experience

Since a later Christianity taught that Jesus was God incarnate, it was perhaps natural to assume that his teaching had come fully formed. Any notion that he had struggled to find the words and the ideas could therefore come as something of a surprise. Yet here in the narrative text of both Matthew and Luke, written before the doctrinal certainties of later centuries, are accounts which show Jesus in deep uncertainty.[32] After the euphoric clarity of the experience at the river Jordan come the doubts, in a sequence which is psychologically convincing for many young people. We can sympathize with him at this early turning point. Perhaps he needs to seek out a place away from the crowds where he can face his own desires and contradictions at a deep level. After all, his later teaching was to challenge the rest of us precisely at our deepest points. Perhaps Jesus' instinctive understanding of this inner world is a witness to his own personal struggle, documented in stylized form in the accounts of three early experiences in the desert.

Some experts think these desert experiences perhaps signal the close of the early phase in which Jesus is content to follow John the Baptist's call to repentance. John seems to have concluded that Jesus was the expected Messiah, who would storm in and separate out the wheat and burn the chaff in an eternal fire. This is the angry rhetoric of national renewal and political liberation, and Jesus' baptism by John seems to hint that at that stage he may still have thought of the Kingdom of Heaven mainly in external, political terms. There is as yet nothing about healing the human condition or the new wine of life or the special role of the outcasts. Jesus' thought is maturing.

The record of the temptations in the desert is like a coded reference to this decisive early phase in the development of his thinking. What tempts him? Three issues are met head-on one after the other, shaping his teaching, deciding what it would *not* be about. In each case the issue evidently takes a long struggle, but the eventual answer when it comes will be central to his teaching. Jesus' teaching will not be about political power; it will not be about material rewards; and it will not be about magic. These are enormous, wide-ranging themes. We can catch here something of the scale of this emerging new vision, the size of this new canvas.

Jesus' reaction to the first temptation, the temptation of political power, is perhaps the clearest indication of his maturing vision. Not all the kingdoms of this world would tempt him, because his vision is not about that kind of power. It is not something that can be ushered in by some edict from the top; it can only work by winning the heart. When it comes to the second temptation, making bread from stones, his reply momentarily sidesteps the bit about magic. Man cannot live from bread alone, he replies; the human heart needs more than that. Today we might add: Not even all the comforts of an affluent lifestyle can truly satisfy the human heart. In the final temptation he is challenged more directly about the use of magic, a force which was very real for people in that culture. Instinctively he's against employing magic because it would be like trying to manipulate God to get what you want.

To us this might seem odd. Generations have seen prayer as partly about asking for something we want, and perhaps this natural human appeal to the heavens occurs to Jesus also, but then suddenly he understands something. In the end all three of the desert temptations are about getting what you want, and in a decisive moment Jesus finally sees through all this to a supreme paradox of the human heart. Liberation, life more abundant, healing the human heart – whatever all this is about, it's not about conventional ideas of power; it's not about getting what you want. The early desert experience has at last brought him a true breakthrough, a true foundation on which he can build.

Can we recognize today the modern equivalents of the three desert temptations? People are still tempted by the lure of power over others and – today perhaps especially – by an addiction to perpetual consumption. Nothing has essentially changed there, but how about the use of magic? Is it going too far to point to the pervasive allure of the modern magicians: today's advertising and entertainment industries? Does this modern trinity, then – power, greed, and the apparatus of wall-to-wall seduction – still sum up the kingdoms of this world today?!

The Limits of Magic

Even today, people who believe in magic in this country and across the world are aware of white magic and black magic – for those who do believe in it, this is still a power you can use for good or ill. Jesus makes his attitude clear in his response in the desert and expands on this elsewhere in the narrative record.[33]

This is worth underlining, since it may well come as a surprise to many people. Signs and wonders prove nothing, says Jesus, because there is no reliable way of telling whether they are from a good or an evil source. In the end you have to judge them by their fruits; that is, you can only trust that they have come from God if you can see that someone has been healed or liberated in some way. Jesus also complains about people who are perpetually waiting for some sensational sign, some wonder which they can chatter about to all their friends.[34] Magic was curiously superficial and was focused very much on getting what you want. So in the end Jesus became more and more wary of the deeply corrupting power of magic, a highly addictive power over people which left them scrambling for security and even less free than they were before. His new teaching, by contrast, aimed at winning over and transforming the heart, for human beings had needs deeper than the material, needs which magic was powerless to provide.

But those around him, including his own followers, were so used to the idea that the supernatural was the clear signal of divinity that his words were apparently not picked up. So those who wrote the Gospel narratives all these years later included not only healing stories but various nature miracles as well, and not least the stories of his birth and resurrection, as the universally accepted signal that this man was no charlatan but someone truly sent from God. Perhaps they forgot that the real test of God's presence is not whether it is accompanied by dazzling magical power, but whether it speaks to the human condition – in the end whether it can heal us.

Today some Christian people still insist that it is necessary to believe the literal truth of the miracle stories. Miracles were a perfectly reasonable thing to believe in then, but the foundations of our beliefs today have changed entirely. It's not just that miracle stories come across to many people today as no more impressive than stage tricks. (Within the last few years television producers have even come up with a series of programs restaging what they call 'Bible tricks'!) Much more important than all that, our universe has been revealed to us in our own time as nothing but miracle, a continuous fabric of breathtaking miracle. This awesomely rational creation teems with wonders which effortlessly make the miracle stories of past times look insignificant.

So it is reassuring to know that Jesus himself, for reasons appropriate to his own time, was no enthusiast for wonder tricks. His message was too serious and too urgent for this kind of distraction. He was aware of a gift for healing within his own tradition, yes, but he was no easy conjurer and there is evidence he hated it when the crowd expected wonders from him. And the Gospel records do not miss the irony of this at his execution. At the very climax of his ministry the expected magic seemed to abandon him, to the amusement of some bystanders. No angels came to rescue him. This poor fool who is supposed to have saved others cannot even save himself, people said, as they shook their heads and turned away.[35]

The Danger of Materialism

Isn't money one of the most deeply paradoxical aspects of human life, time after time setting off strong feelings and deep-set alarm bells? There are probably few topics like it for probing under the surface of the human heart. Recently a financial writer went so far as to say that 'money is more intimate than sex, sought with more passion than true love, defining our innermost selves'.[36] It seems to be close to a tender point inside us, linked to our ever-present search for security and inner worth.

According to recent figures, the per capita annual income of Nigeria is $860, that of Turkey is $5,430, and that of the UK is $39,750.[37] The disparity is striking. However, a good deal of the spectacular rise in the wealth of the West and of Japan has happened since the end of the Second World War, that is, in living memory of older people still alive today. Much of it is recent. Today this process appears to be taking off in China and in the Far East, in India, in Russia, and at varying rates in parts of Latin America. At this rate, by the time today's children have reached middle years, the really poor nations could quite possibly be confined mainly to sub-Saharan Africa and isolated cases scattered about the other continents – and more recently in parts of Africa, too, a new hope is arising. Yes, there will be all sorts of problems along the way, many of these no doubt something to do with naked greed and power, but despite all these it does look distinctly possible that most nations on earth will achieve some measure of affluence within little more than 50 years from now, or at most between 50 and a hundred. That's if we succeed in limiting population growth, curb our greed and manage to avoid major wars or serious environmental damage in the meantime!

Seen from where we are today, this spread of affluence seems like an event of the first magnitude in human history. Eradicating poverty worldwide, until recently only a dream, has begun to seem a realizable goal to set ourselves, and this raises enormous hopes, creating opportunities and widening horizons for people in all continents. Poverty is perhaps man-made after all, and not a state of nature. At the same time, money on a large scale without effective mechanisms of political control can be the most lethal undiluted curse you could wish on your worst enemy. The horrendous realities of the drugs trade or prostitution-trafficking worldwide can witness to that. Money, power and greed do seem to combine together especially easily within us, almost like a strong chemical bond, potentially a true trinity of evil in the human heart.

For the individual, too, money can be a blessing or a curse or a mixture of both. A certain minimum level of income makes it possible to live in the dignity which is surely the birthright of every one of us. Give us this day our daily bread, says the great prayer. Who would disapprove of the freedom to spend generously on a friend, say, or the sense of safety provided by a level of financial security?

And yet there is undeniably something very strange about money, a kind of India-rubber, surreal quality, a world away from common sense. What other commodity has the quality that we never have quite enough? What other stuff can so seduce us into believing that it really can satisfy the heart, but in reality hardly ever does for very long? Even more peculiar, people can often surround money with fantasies and dreams, with delusions and self-deceptions, and it can become so private that we sometimes find it hard to be completely honest even with ourselves about it. The desire for money and what it can buy is also inherently inflationary, so it seems. It grows and feeds on itself, like something organic. Meanwhile the suspicion that we are on a treadmill occasionally does occur to us. There is something very odd about all this, something under the surface and just out of reach of our conscious attention. The more we get, the more we seem to need. How very strange.

Most crucially, though, money can lure us little by little into becoming preoccupied with ourselves, and it can build invisible walls around us which cause the external world with all its wonders to subtly fade from our attention. And in doing this, can it not be gorgeously seductive?

Jesus' teaching on money is emphatic but at the same time subtle and challenging. We can tell from some of his parables that Jesus was probably quite used to money. He tells stories of rich merchants going on business journeys, of farmers paying day workers, of merchants buying pearls and of fathers dividing their inheritance, all perfectly naturally and without disapproval of money as such. He himself is pictured again and again feasting and drinking with people, and he wanders the country for an extended period of time, apparently without needing to earn his own living. Paul apparently thinks he was originally quite well off but had become poor voluntarily.[38] All of this hints at a family background free of the desperation of real poverty.

He is used to money but wary of it. 'Do not store up for yourselves treasure on earth, where moth and rust destroy, and thieves break in and steal,' he says.[39] He has seen through it. He sees that money is part of the generosity of the creation and it can enlarge our freedom and bring us satisfaction, but little by little it can also capture us, undermining the very freedom and fullness which we thought we had set out to find. He seems to be saying, It's a gift – go ahead and enjoy it thankfully, but pay attention to its strangely compulsive power over us. A degree of affluence, in itself perfectly legitimate, can be a lethal distraction from that birthright, that completion of our nature which alone can finally give us peace and bring us home. 'No one can serve two masters; for either he will hate the first and love the second, or he will be devoted to the first and despise the second. You cannot serve God and Money.'[40] This is a strong statement and it fits closely with his wariness of all social and political power.

A young man comes up to Jesus, respectfully calls him 'Master', and asks him what he needs to do to inherit eternal life[41] – 'inherit' eternal life, the translation favoured by the Authorized Version, almost treats it as if it were some kind of legal property right. This man seems to have everything he could ever want, but evidently still misses something. Maybe he is a bit of a charmer, used to getting his way with people. Jesus tests him on the commandments. He has kept them all since childhood, he says. At this point Jesus hesitates and the young man seems momentarily mystified. Hasn't he done everything he can to earn eternal life? Doesn't he deserve it? Then suddenly Jesus says, All right, if you are really serious about this, sell all you have and give it to the poor, and then come and follow me, and you shall have treasure in heaven – 'treasure', like a bank account in credit. He echoes the questioner's vocabulary back to him, apparently with a conscious irony! At that, the young man goes away with a heavy heart (one account tells us that his face fell), for as the narrative puts it, he was a man of great wealth. You cannot serve two masters.

It seems so natural, doesn't it? The more we have, the more we put our security and our trust in what we have. 'For where your treasure is, there will your heart be also,' says Jesus.[42] But we can't secure the elixir of life by trying to earn it! This is not about getting something we want. In fact it does seem that getting what we want can often blind us to seeing what we really need at a deeper level. The theme of human blindness keeps cropping up in the four narratives.

Characteristically Jesus goes deeper than we expected, shrewdly putting his finger on something we don't often like to dwell on. If life stubbornly fails to make any kind of sense, it is so human to take refuge in pleasure, in consuming, in the kind of things that money can buy. These can undoubtedly comfort us, but perhaps with a counterfeit comfort. They comfort us and in the same instant they distract us from this deeper, altogether more fundamental agenda of making sense of things. Assuredly this kind of comfort is not what life is about.

This is a highly distinctive teaching about the danger of money and its fundamental incompatibility with the urgent business of attaining our birthright, the completion of our nature, something which we are born searching for. This insight, moreover, hangs together with other insights, for example the wariness of hierarchies and the human lust for power, or the too-easy use of violence in human affairs, and the poisonous consequences of doing so. Yet these teachings are today only slowly being brought back to the core of Christian understanding. For long, they have been widely held in polite contempt, at best an option for the high-minded, but in no sense taken seriously as an essential part of the call to follow Jesus.

Politics and the Human Conundrum

Jesus' very choice of metaphor – a Kingdom – for his central idea places him in a broad stream of thought which aspired to free Israel. This is an important reason why his teaching could be so easily misunderstood, both by potential followers and by the authorities. Even as late as his trial, Jesus had to protest that his Kingdom was not of this world, and with supreme irony it may have been partly because of the widespread confusion about what his teaching did mean that he was eventually led to his execution. The problem was that there was a logic linking Jesus' ideas and the idea of political liberation, and this was widely understood at the time. Israel would only be liberated when its people had repented and turned to their God, so repentance would be the forerunner of a successful national uprising against the Roman power.

This is what makes Jesus' desert decision to reject the ends and means of the world of politics a decision of the first rank of importance, and incidentally stands out as authentically his own teaching. People around him, including people who sympathized with him, kept assuming quite naturally that it was all partly about political liberation. Was it this vital shift of emphasis away from national liberation, from saving Israel, which eventually persuaded Judas to turn against his leader and betray him? This would mean, ironically, that his arrest and execution were tied up with this crucial shift away from politics, catching him between some disappointed, angry followers and the political authority they had hoped he would lead them against!

Teaching found in the Jewish scriptures came to mind. Every valley shall be exalted, every mountain and hill made low; the first shall be last and the last first. For Jesus, the contrast between the two kingdoms soon became absolute and fundamental. One appealed to humanity's baser instincts like fear and greed, and used hierarchical systems of authority backed up where necessary by violence. The inner Kingdom appealed to quite other, deeper aspirations within the heart and in principle couldn't ever employ such methods. If it did so, it simply wouldn't be the Kingdom of Heaven. So the contrast between the two kingdoms was built into human nature itself. Yet things were not simple. The point was not to condemn the kingdoms of this world; they were what they were. Caesar must be allowed his coin; human authority was necessary. The good news of the new Kingdom still asserted human worth, still cared about justice and hoped for a transformed human society – all part of the prophetic tradition which Jesus inherited and took forward. It's just that Caesar's ways had no affinity with God's ways.

Today's democratic politics seem to be a world away from the ways of the early empires. To some degree or other we are all democrats now. Politics at its best has been rightly called the noble art of the possible, yet the methods and aspirations of politics today are, I suspect, just as easily corrupted as they were then. Assuredly, politicians are not 'all the same', as is often claimed. There are good people in politics with honorable aspirations, but the urgent logic of persuasion and the drive for power can make it dauntingly hard over the years to tell truth from plausibility, reality from spin. So much of politics is about trade-offs, compromises and the tyranny of short-term considerations, and the influence of business and the media is pervasive. Who controls whom? And with power and time come the dangers of arrogance and cynicism. Power corrupts, all right.

But this goes further. Human nature and human need are contradictory and complex, and Jesus' vision sees further than humanitarian ideals, reaching parts they simply cannot reach. It's not just that the methods of politics are so easily corruptible; it's that its aims, too, only take us so far. In brief, eradicating poverty is a noble aim, but once you have succeeded in achieving it, what then? Economic justice is necessary, but is affluence really enough to satisfy the longings of the heart? In the stylized account of Jesus' time in the desert, large questions were worked through which set a framework for later insights. It was in the desert that Jesus saw most clearly the contradiction built into human nature, and how power and ego actually got in the way, blinding us to our deeper birthright, the elixir of life, that which could finally make us whole.

But evidence keeps cropping up within the four narratives that plenty of Jesus' followers kept on thinking that the Kingdom was itself political in some literal sense.[43] One of the twelve disciples was known as Simon the Zealot – the Zealots were part of a resistance movement started around the time of Jesus' birth. There is even speculation that the name Judas Iscariot is a corruption of Judas Sicarius – the *sicarii* were the 'sickle men', terrorists who went in for assassination by use of the curved blade! This association of the Kingdom with some expected political outcome persisted. As Jesus rides into town on the back of an ass, the crowds are shouting for the kingdom of David to return.[44] ('Hosanna', incidentally, means not 'Hurrah' but 'we pray'!) An anti-Roman element was apparently a feature of early Christianity right through the first century and beyond.

At Jesus' trial this ambiguity crops up yet again. We are probably familiar with Pilate's offer to the crowd: 'Which shall I release to you, Jesus or Barabbas?', but in Matthew's account it reads with a quite different edge to it. 'Which would you like me to release to you – Jesus Barabbas, or Jesus called Messiah?'[45] Barabbas means literally 'son of the father', a name redolent with meaning for all who knew Jesus' teaching. But Luke's account tells us that this Barabbas had been put in prison for murder committed as part of a rising in the city – political unrest still hovering behind the narrative.[46] Seen in this light, Jesus Barabbas is almost like the alter ego of Jesus called Messiah. Matthew's text here has a quite extraordinary candor. It's as if the narrator is himself unsure which of the two to choose, so he turns round and passes the challenge directly to the reader. Which Jesus do you believe, then? Which Kingdom do you want: the Kingdom which comes about through an inspired military uprising, or the Kingdom which conquers the heart?

Chapter 6
The Kingdom Deep Within

Speaking to the Heart

One immediately striking feature of Jesus is that time and again he recommends us to be immoderate, surely an eloquent witness that this was a young man's vision. Right at the core of his teaching is this sense that there is a key to living, and it's not obvious. It's not on the surface, so it's worth searching for, and if you find it, quite simply it's worth everything you have. This extraordinary paradox is placed right at the heart of his teaching, and this is expressed in the mini-story of the pearl of great price, in which a merchant, when he suddenly finds the pearl, sells all that he has and buys it.[47] This doesn't exactly sound like a counsel of prudence; in fact Jesus' teaching at first glance does seem to have an air of naive idealism about it. When the time comes, don't be afraid – jump! This is about trust, and it's also about the secret of life. He understands that human nature is all the while looking around for a way out of its fears and uncertainties.

Right at the start, then, we are presented with perhaps the central paradox of human nature. We do want to find the key to life, but we are constantly distracted by the details and the temptations of living, and deep inside quite understandably we're perhaps afraid. Could wild horses ever persuade us to embark on such an uncertain enterprise as the search for the key to life? Torn between desire and fear – is that what it is to be human? Is that really us? So often, Jesus touches on things we would rather not have to think about, parts of us which are perhaps just too tender to face. He confronts us with our own limits and vulnerability, and one part of us maybe flares up in anger. Who does this young man think he is?! And another part of us quietly listens, maybe hearing a bell ringing somewhere inside us.

In a number of places the narrative Gospels catch the authentic urgency, freshness and impatience of this man's vision. Characteristically it is strikingly simple. Don't worry about tomorrow, he says. Take each day as it comes; you're in good hands. 'Easily said,' we might reply. 'Positively scary to really do.' Is it possible that Jesus underrates what we might call the 'skepticism of experience' among his older hearers? His youth is a part of his message, and the core of his message is trust. This teaching is not as simple as it looks, either. Somewhere inside us we'd give our right arm to be able to take each day as it comes.

There is one persistent question which preoccupied people in classical times and still does today, reflecting a profound lack of trust in the events of life. How do you attract good fortune and avoid bad fortune, and if your God or your good luck angel has anything to do with it, how can you get him on side? Conversely, if bad luck does strike, what have you (or your ancestors) done to deserve it? We can recognize this. In some circles today it is fashionable to talk about karma. It's about the search for a way out of the uncertainty of living. Jesus makes several responses to this theme, and in doing this he doesn't impose any single 'right answer'. He simply shares a vision and invites us to see it, aware that not everyone will do so. It's not about reasoning; it goes deeper. It's about seeing, and there's an element of our own choice involved in this.

First, although there are times when we really do reap what we sow, at other times things don't turn out how we expected. Surprises do happen, and we describe them with words like grace or good fortune, but these events are in the end a mystery. Bafflingly, this God seems to distribute his bounty without any reliable rhyme or reason. We need only look around us. He causes his sun to shine on the just and unjust, decent folk and complete bastards, with equal favor.

Second, in one of his most vivid insights Jesus reflects on this apparently scandalous conclusion and sees that the generosity of nature is simply overwhelming, like the sunlight. The bounty of nature simply pours over us and around us all the time, yet people are almost always blind to it. Several well-known verses illustrate this teaching. The hairs on your head are numbered, he says. Two sparrows can be sold for five farthings, yet your heavenly father watches over even them. Consider the lilies of the fields: they don't have to earn their living yet even the great king Solomon was not clothed in such style.[48] Here is a vision, unusual for its time, which suddenly sees the teeming generosity of the creation and sees that even the most everyday events of our lives are flooded by it. We are absolutely in good hands. Just for a moment, it can suddenly seem reasonable after all to stop worrying and to simply trust providence for your needs for the day. This of course is part of the Lord's Prayer.[49] It is very central, and yet it does occur to us that it is apparently too simple, not to say unwise. Again the paradox of desire and fear is not far away.

Third, we all know that people are seeking after security and happiness all the time, but time and again in the wrong places! We seem to be programmed to get it wrong. You can't get it from possessions; they are a trap. They are so very tempting, yet ultimately they don't answer our search. What is the point of gaining the whole world and losing yourself? The business of accumulating wealth and power can be so addictive that you may lose the way back to your real self; you may forget what it is to be real. So where is this security to be found? It can be found in a life lived in trust and contentment with what you are given, in God's Kingdom of the heart, in a life lived in love with every day and in forgiveness with the people around you. Yet again, at first it sounds so simple and naive that we think it can't possibly be right.

Jesus' fourth response is the hardest to say, because it hits a tender spot for so many of us: Even if you have to go through bad times, carry on trusting through the suffering as much as you are able. Even though I go through the valley of the shadow of death, yet will I fear no evil. Whatever happens – *whatever* happens – be still and know that you are a child of providence, of this overwhelming creation. And strangest of all to say, although suffering can just be miserable with nothing to relieve it, on occasion it can bring forth unexpected fruits, like courage, commitment, a deeper understanding of another person, the consolation of sharing and the relief of tears – all epiphanies of grace. Blessed are those who mourn – they shall see God. Some of the very deepest points of life have to do with either joy or suffering. Such are the mysterious depths of human experience.

But we know perfectly well that sometimes these things don't happen, and that suffering is perhaps the bleakest of all the mysteries of life. Had Jesus' teaching been handing down a series of ready-made doctrines, totally confident cut-and-dried answers for every question, it would have had the effect of dismissing our suffering, explaining it away. Instead he recognizes the importance of simple human solidarity when faced with this mystery of our existence. The healing stories are marked by respect for those concerned. Over and over again he tells people it's their own faith which has healed them. Just like his teaching through stories, nothing is imposed; it's up to us to react to it or not. Growth and healing come from deep inside us.

Characteristically Jesus doesn't just theorize. He actually seeks out the misfits and the outcasts and eats and drinks with them, so much so indeed that he is severely criticized for associating with such unsavory people. Some commentators point out that the purpose of relating the healing miracles in the four Gospels was not so much that they were miracles but that they were about bringing people back into community, and perhaps above all they were about touching people. The Jewish religion, like other religions of that time, listed many categories of people who were regarded as ritually unclean, whom no serious religious person would ever come near, let alone actually come into contact with. It is said that the four Gospel narrators between them cover just about every possible category on this lengthy list, including the blind, lepers, the sick, the spiritually troubled or deranged, but also prostitutes, money changers, tax gatherers, menstruating women and many, many more. In these encounters Jesus goes out of his way to touch people, declaring by doing so their inclusion in the community of God's children. At the time, this was a sensational, provocative act, for some an outrage causing great offense, and for those affected a dramatic act of acceptance.

The Gangster

He befriends not just those whom we might call the innocent poor; he includes anyone who is rejected by others, even the hated tax gatherers. This was a class of people feared and loathed by those around them, people who routinely used threats and violence, robbing the poor in the service of the despised Roman authority. You could say they were gangsters, the *mafiosi* of their day. Luke tells us that Zacchaeus, a tax gatherer, had climbed into a tree because he had wanted to see Jesus but was small of stature.[50] Perhaps there is more to it than this. Aware of his own despised, unclean status, he probably imagines that Jesus and his followers in the crowd will not want to come anywhere near him. So he wants to see but not be seen.

How does Jesus react ? He has not missed the fact that this man has gone to some trouble to make sure he can see him. Suddenly he sees the problem. Stop hiding in that tree, Zacchaeus, he says. Tonight I'm eating at your house! At a stroke he offers a dramatic acceptance to an outcast, courageously expressing a belief in him which no doubt runs against the strongly felt anti-Roman views of those around him. This hard-bitten cynic is so gobsmacked at this that he nearly falls out of the tree, and soon finds himself promising to repay fourfold anything he has taken unjustly and to sell one half of his goods and give to the poor. This is quite a promise, a true emotional landslide within him, set off when this man so unexpectedly declares him accepted, in effect forgiven.

Notice that he is not accepted on condition that he first of all reform himself. The logic is the other way round: he is forgiven first, simply and unconditionally, and when this dawns on him it moves him so much that he freely promises to reform himself root and branch. Such is the unexpected, upside-down logic of the creator's love as seen by Jesus. So even a dangerous man so habituated to violence, a lost soul like Zacchaeus, isn't beyond the reach of this overarching love.

And this story, like so many of the healing stories, illustrates a characteristic feature of Jesus: an instinct for a dramatic gesture which needs hardly any words, rather like his response to the young woman who bathed his feet in her tears. This man has a distinctive, highly economical style of his own.

Logic in the Unconscious

What is the logic behind this consciously paradoxical teaching and this deliberate public notoriety? It's the poor, the outcasts, those who suffer who will desperately cast around for help, not the comfortable, not the complacent or smug or self-righteous. In the devastating words of the narrative, they 'have their reward' already. After all, why should the self-satisfied look for help? The rewards of this life have blinded them to any other reality.

This is the psychological insight behind the idea that God's heart goes out especially to anyone who suffers. There is an inner truth there, an inner paradox of human experience which we can recognize. Power and comfort can bring complacency, while trouble can sometimes concentrate the mind and bring clarity. This is a sophisticated, subtle insight about human nature, an insight which maybe doesn't always apply every single time but which rings true nevertheless. And although this insight is deceptively simple on the surface, it carries a message of immense power in all ages. Just think how African slaves in the new world responded to this friend of the friendless.

Time and again, behind Jesus' teaching there lies a deeper psychological insight. This is perhaps most clearly true for the teaching on forgiveness. If you don't forgive others yourself, you won't be forgiven, he says. This is not about a cold, resentful God; it's a truth of the inner Kingdom. Forgiving is sometimes exceptionally hard to do honestly, and it demands its own time. There is a mechanism within us justifying our anger, and which of us on any one occasion can say it's not valid? But when it is given to us eventually to forgive, it comes from a point deep inside us. This is sometimes accompanied by a characteristic liberating rush of emotion coming to us suddenly like an unaccountable blessing.

And the ultimate reality of Jesus' vision, the framework within which he sees everything else, is that we are all children of his God's overwhelming creation. When we realize that we are cared for in such astonishing detail, everything suddenly is transformed and new things become possible. Notice that this is the experience of something which we are initially blind to, something which logic cannot reach on its own. But all the while in the dynamic inner Kingdom, under the surface of consciousness, there is something working away within us which can create new understanding apparently from nothing.

Jesus' vision gets below the resistance mechanisms of the mind; hence the characteristic delay before it is given to us to see it, and although there is an unmistakable urgency in his teaching, there is also a trust in human nature. When the stakes are this high it is maybe quite reasonable to be wary of any teaching which promises so much. Nevertheless the truth of this teaching echoes deep in the heart, and given time, plenty of people will recognize it. Jesus compares this to a farmer sowing seeds. Some seeds will fall on stony ground; others will grow and flourish, bringing in a rich harvest. The model is of trust in a natural process.

Where does the startling authority of Jesus' teaching come from? He speaks with a fiercely uncompromising honesty about uncomfortable things which habitually we screen off. Instinctively we resist, yet somewhere within we may find ourselves hesitating. We can see that it's about the elixir of life, the ultimate prize.

There is a repeated pattern in this teaching: an often arresting paradox built in, a telling accuracy and depth behind a surface of apparent, even baffling, simplicity. We are encountering a distinctive understanding of the human heart, which cuts through logic, freeing the imagination. With exceptional clarity he sees the contradictory forces within us and our search for the secret of life. He shows us the indescribable generous beauty of the creation and sees it as witness that we are loved. When we see that, when we truly digest it, new things can become possible. Jesus is evidently not as naive as he seemed to be at first hearing, and it's the unconscious dimension to his teaching, its unexpected depth, which can allow us to make sense out of it.

But this teaching goes further and wider, and other themes interlock together within its encompassing vision, illuminating more of the recesses of the mind. The next four chapters will examine some of these themes in turn, shedding more light on this teaching, each from a different angle. The thing is, Jesus aims to elicit from us more than just respect; his aim is to persuade us into the adventure of following him. But his own respect for us too is equally evident. He shares a vision with us, he invites us to follow, and then he leaves it up to us to respond (or not) in our own way. It won't come alive unless we make it come alive.

Chapter 7
Love Transfigured

Love and Violence

Ancient pagan traditions recognized something we can call love, a demonic spirit within the human heart, a divine madness capable of transforming us as if by magic, transforming how we are and what becomes possible for us. This could bring a fleeting taste of paradise, a taste to die (or kill) for, but at the same time it could wreak fearful damage, partly because it could lead to alliances and wars. If my enemy's enemy is my friend, my friend's enemy can also quickly become my enemy. Love's awesome alchemy could work both ways.

An appeal to something very like love is basic in the training of any modern army. If men are going to risk their lives for each other, you have to first of all build a remarkably close relationship among them. In our embarrassed, neurotic age, men don't like to talk about loving each other, but the strong bond between men which makes an army effective surely behaves very like a form of love. (Field Marshall Slim is said to have said of commanding a platoon, 'You must know your men better than their mothers, and love them just as much.')

Sexual and family love have some of the same characteristics. Isn't it especially vulnerable precisely because it affects our most intimate hopes and needs, stirring yearnings within us which come from our very deepest levels? By its very nature it is exclusive, fostering a powerful delusion that you and those you love are the very center of the universe, and yet it can release a transcendent generosity back to the whole universe, a solidarity with all lovers and all parents and their children. But human anger and human grief know no bounds when this love is damaged or taken away.

Paradoxical as it may sound, love is very much part of the human problem. Love is dangerous. If a perceived enemy has harmed one of your own, or even if you have been persuaded that they might do so in the future, the veneer of civilized behavior can vanish like snow on a wall, and heinous crimes can be committed in a spirit of righteous hatred for outsiders, as we know especially well in recent history. As the saying goes, in love and war, all is fair. Humans can experience a real buzz from the adventure of defending their world against perceived threats, an adventure in which open aggression and violence can suddenly be permitted. And societies heap such adulation on victorious soldiers! Think of the countless stories recycled in modern films, from war stories to westerns, spy thrillers to fantasy epics. The adventure of war is as glamorous as it ever was.

Yet the problem of love and war might soon enough destroy us. In fact it is the menacing logic of war itself which may now require us to reassess everything from the bottom up – our needs, ambitions, fears, all the causes of conflict – and to learn exceptionally quickly to develop a new sophistication, a new wisdom which will at least allow us to survive. Other species have achieved this, have found ways to defuse aggression, and now the challenge has come to us.

I think Jesus' teaching may have an important comment to make on this, because it is about understanding a new kind of love, about seeing ourselves from a wider perspective, and about achieving things which at first sight seem impossible.

Seeing Beyond the Conundrum

Why should we take the trouble to love our neighbor? Is it hard-wired in us? Forming friendships does seem to be one of our deepest needs, and altruistic acts can take us out of ourselves. In a strange way it isn't really in our own self-interest to look after our own self-interest all the time! Helping others can be interesting and rewarding, especially if the person we're helping is pretty, or deserving, or touchingly grateful, or one of us. But what about those who are not pretty, not deserving, not grateful or not one of us? Quite often this is what sets limits to our willingness to help, and this brings us back to in-groups and out-groups, a basic feature of human society in all ages. Urging us to love some people seems like asking for pigs to fly; it seems just perfectly naive. Loving, like forgiving, like belief itself, is not something you can command.

What Jesus means by 'love' is apparently something thoughtful and steadfast precisely because it is *not* forced, because in a way it comes naturally. But how can that be? The kind of love Jesus seems to have in mind is more than just a willingness to help, which can come and go; it is something steadier and more committed, less dependent on mood or circumstance. What he actually says comes in two halves, and the first half is often forgotten: '… you must love the Lord your God with all your heart, with all your soul, with all your mind, and with all your strength.' And 'love your neighbour as yourself.'[51] Jesus is quoting the Shema, the Jewish declaration of faith. At first sight this seems implausible to some modern minds because of the difficulty many people today have with the idea of God. (In Chapter 16 we'll come back to this question.)

Perhaps the key to the riddle is that Jesus links this commandment with a quite separate one about loving your neighbor. It seems to be saying that if you can love your God in this extraordinary way with all your heart and all your strength and all your mind, then you will find that you will also love your neighbor as yourself quite naturally. Either the one will lead to the other, or else they are in some sense perhaps the same thing anyway.

Love cannot be commanded but it can seize us, sometimes unexpectedly, apparently following its own logic. So loving our enemies isn't something we can be compelled to do, but it can come to us. Sometimes we can be struck, as by Cupid's arrow, with a sudden beauty and we see the blessing and sheer gift of life. As we saw in the previous chapter, Jesus points to the overwhelming generosity of nature, something which we usually don't notice. One part of us wishes that we could somehow see things from a wider, cooler perspective; then on occasion it can strike us with sudden clarity.

If our creator cares for us with such passionate enthusiasm, expressed so amply in the endless details of our surrounding creation, doesn't this confer on us the dignity and the fundamental equality of the creation itself? And doesn't this new light expose the vanity of all social pretension, class privilege, inequality and all oppression of the human heart? Suddenly we see ourselves and our neighbor in an entirely new light.

The Heart's Desire

A key part of the authentic genius of Jesus is that he sees that human beings just ache for love and for respect. How many of us spend years of our lives under the fear that perhaps we aren't worth very much after all? This can cripple people, ruining the potential they have to live creative, abundant lives, free of this constantly dogging uncertainty and fear. It has been suggested that the reason why people often treat money in such bizarre, irrational ways is because of this great chasm in the middle of their lives. Perhaps money is the great substitute for the thing they are searching for and can't find. This is what Jesus' teaching taps into, this intuition that deep down human beings would give anything to find this secret to living freely and fully.

Wouldn't it somehow be typically human if it turned out that all the time we had been blind to something which in reality was surrounding us on all sides?! Despite this customary blindness to it, the sheer detail and generosity of our creation is truly overwhelming. Either you see this or you don't, but if you do, the experience is unmistakable. Like suddenly being able to forgive someone for the first time, somewhere inside us a blockage will have been freed, and instinctively we will know that this is an important moment.

It is when we are freed to love life truly with all our strength, and love ourselves in the same way, that loving our neighbor can suddenly seem the most natural thing in the world. All at once it seems obviously realistic. This is about seeing the bigger picture, not just our familiar social reality but an altogether wider creation into which this human drama is set. And this new perspective, this wider truth we couldn't see before, really can give us the sensation of being set free. It can even strike us that we must have been blind as bats before. Just, indeed, like falling in love. Precisely. Falling in love with the whole of life, the whole damn' circus.

It has been said that if we like or dislike someone this is often because we unconsciously see in them aspects of ourselves which we like or dislike. Perceiving people can be like looking in a mirror, and as soon as human beings start to dislike one another, be it individuals or nations, dishonesty soon rears its head as we project all the negatives, all the blame and responsibility, onto them and away from ourselves. But it's our own insecurity which drives this whole mechanism, isn't it? This new vision honestly faces this and can provide an antidote to it.

This new way of seeing people doesn't require us to suppress our honest view of someone we don't like, but if we can see them and ourselves, flaws and all, at one and the same time, then we may be able to laugh and forgive them and ourselves together – all members of this perfectly incorrigible, wonderfully imperfect species. There is no need to be naive, no need to kid ourselves. This new vision is about a wider truth; it's about understanding more, seeing further than we did before.

This is Jesus' answer to the problem of love and human aggression, this glory of human nature which threatens to destroy us in our own time. This is a way, not so much of taming love but of universalizing it so that there are no more out-groups.

Suddenly we can see ourselves within an infinitely wider and more inspiring frame, a frame in which our reality expands in a single leap of the imagination to embrace our entire creation. Every one of us is made with such overwhelming generosity and care – we are so jewel-like – that it now can seem a heinous crime ever to harm another person.

Has not this very vision already been influential in the politics of the last two centuries? Isn't this one of the crucial insights behind the entire modern human rights movement? Now perhaps we just need to take the emotional logic of this vision a bit further towards its own natural conclusion. Human beings as a species have a powerful learning capacity. When they see things differently, they really can change the way they act, and this really can solve what previously seemed like insoluble problems. If the demonic power of love can be understood and transfigured, then perhaps its famous divine alchemy, its long-recognized power to transform us, can finally save us from ourselves. Truly this is epic stuff, capable one day, who knows, of changing the course of human history.

Chapter 8
Dying and Living

All Things Pass Away

'Of an early death the cricket sang,' wrote an early Buddhist poet, sensing the pathos of all created things. People in eastern religious traditions have pictured the creation as one continuing dance in which all things are born, flourish, decline and die, and in which everything is recycled, creating to the end of time itself a continuous newness, freshness and youth. Living things express this transience particularly vividly but mountain ranges and planets and galaxies dance just as surely.[52] There are quick dances and slow ones, simple dances and impenetrably complex ones, but all of them are part of the dazzling, stupendous dance of a creation whose passing beauty and pathos can catch the heart.

A traditional Zen dialogue expresses the startling wonder of the passing moment like this:

All things pass away.
'Yes, but feel the quiet magic of this dawn!'
All things pass away.
'Yes, but look at this dreamlike snowstorm swirling outside my window!'
All things pass away.
'Yes, but listen to the blackbird singing on the rooftop this late spring evening!'

The beauty of all things seems to be enhanced and intensified by their very transience, and even the times of day and the seasons of the year echo this fleeting hidden beauty. There is indeed a pathos to all things, a pity, an irony, a richness to all this explosive beauty on all sides mysteriously dancing to the beat of time passing, apparently to no discernible purpose or point. All of this can move us with a strange awe.

As far as we know, Jesus did not actually teach that beauty and transience are linked. But if beauty is tied up with the transience of all things around us, is this not also true for us and our lives as well? It's not as if we are space travelers from somewhere else, observing this creation through a glass window. We are born out of it, like leaves on a tree; we are its children, and its wonders cascade around us and right through us. We are very much part of what we observe, and yet we too are temporary visitors, temporary witnesses to this awesome spectacle. On reflection, Jesus' lyrical teaching of the overwhelming generosity of the creation does come reasonably close to this, and his teaching about our place in this creation is also linked with another part of his teaching, about the oneness of living and dying.

In one of Gulliver's travels in the tales by Jonathan Swift, the hero visits a world in which people are unable to die. As century follows century they are quite overcome by a listless sadness and depression, and Gulliver is glad to get away from them. There seems to be a rightness about being born, living out our span, and then dying, and true tragedy occurs when this wholeness is cut short. Attempts by individuals to extend their youth beyond all due proportion or to even deep-freeze their remains in the hope of some future bodily resurrection can seem to us pathetic and sad. The beauty of each stage of life depends on a definite time-limited quality of the whole thing in which each stage plays its role in a wider unity. Children and young people have a special kind of innocence and blind energy which even at times can enact a very good imitation of immortality (just for a while!), but older people can see them with an affectionate irony when they remember their own youth, for old age is full of irresistible memory. There is a roundness to all this, a naturalness to life as a whole, and strange to say, dying in old age does seem to be part of life's unaccountable blessing.

The trouble is that throughout most of our lives we are so preoccupied with worries and uncertainties that we may find it very hard indeed to relax and appreciate the great fullness and richness of the gift of life. It's almost as if we have been crippled, or blinded, or locked up in some prison, unable to truly live, to truly enjoy this gift. If only we could somehow learn to open up to life, to trust it and accept it, and escape from these constant, pestering anxieties.

Behind Jesus' teaching is a vision that the gift of life which we are given when we are born is so overwhelming that it effortlessly excels all that we ourselves can ever work to earn, all our strenuous efforts and achievements. Perhaps it was this vision which lay behind his apparently simple advice to us to accept life as it comes, to live for each day and stop worrying. To say that most of us most of the time underrate the beauty of the gift of life is surely an understatement. The great generous gift is under our noses and most of the time we are just too busy to notice it.

It does seem to be our constantly driving ego which so often gets in the way of a more open, trusting approach to the experience of being alive. Perhaps we need to permit ourselves some freedom from always having to get what we want, always having to be right all the time. Then at last we might see the possibility of a richer experience of life. It's as if ego and trust are somehow opposites, one getting in the way of the other.

Appetite and Loss

The consistent teaching of Jesus, so far from disapproving of the rich blessings of life, encourages us to enjoy them and be thankful for them. Jesus himself was known as a reveler, feasting, eating and drinking with people, in somewhat stark contrast to his erstwhile mentor, John the Baptist, for whom an ascetic life seems to have been central. So it seems that Jesus was no ascetic. (This is important, for he is frequently seen as just exactly that.)

Jesus appears to be saying, Gratefully enjoy life's gifts but learn to be wise to yourself and be especially wary of addictions, that is, anything which can easily narrow and impoverish the full breadth of your enjoyment of life. The example which springs to mind today is of course hard drugs, which can indeed dramatically take us over like a virus and ruin everything around us. But this is just one extreme example of a much more general weakness which seems to be built into human nature and which can damage our experience of life. It does begin to look as if all of the gifts of life are double-edged; they all seem to present us with a challenge. This can be unnerving to some people, tempting them either to shut down on pleasure or else to indulge themselves too far, or perhaps to do both alternately, in quick manic succession! It seems that an out-of-control ego goes hand-in-hand with an underlying fear. This ego inside us seems to need an antidote, a countervailing principle to govern it and set us free from our fear.

As the Buddha in another culture discovered, all desire, all enjoyment whatsoever, carries with it a shadow, namely, the fear of loss. Experience something pleasurable or attractive, even something spiritually satisfying, and we will instinctively want to ensure that we can experience it again; hence the instinct to pin it down, to have it under our control. This is the root of something which if left unchecked can turn out pretty imprisoning: human appetite, a preoccupation with self in which life becomes a process of having and consuming. And what happens when we pin a desirable experience down, so we can have it again and again? Doesn't it very often eventually lose its freshness, and go stale, and run like sand through our fingers? The law of fading satisfaction eventually starts to kick in, and the fear of loss is usually not far away. This looks like a neurosis built in to human nature.

And yet, and yet... The intriguing thing is that this law is evidently not universal. Some relationships change and deepen; some things we appreciate more deeply and with better understanding over time. These exceptions seem to be connected with learning and with something we can call human wisdom, a process of growing into wholeness.

Still, human beings do seem to form delusions or addictions of some kind or other, and so often it takes a surprise or a loss of some kind to jolt us back into a sense of our wider reality. As a species we certainly seem to be programmed to lose the big picture again and again. More consumption doesn't bring more happiness. We know that perfectly well, but it sure does promise to do so, and we are so easily seduced! Pleasure of all kinds carries this shadow, the fear of loss.

Why do we indulge in such apparently endless consumption? The history of economics and politics is dominated by variations on human greed. Perhaps this is not because it actually does bring us the satisfaction we crave, but precisely because it *fails* to do so. We cannot for the life of us see anything better, so round we go on our treadmill again.

Healing the Human Condition

Jesus' view of this perpetually frustrating search for the secret of living is of a sickness needing to be healed, but he never gives the impression that this sickness is incurable. Right throughout the four Gospels the emphasis is on healing and freeing people. The root of our sickness seems to be fear, and maybe the key to overcoming that fear is the conviction that we really are loved and our response to that love, the lifelong agenda of learning to trust. Maybe this *can* seduce us away from worshipping our ego quite so much, and by doing this can conquer the pervasive fear which seems to accompany the ego like a shadow.

It's not that fear is always bad. In many situations fear can be a friend, warning us what to avoid, but fear which grows out of all proportion can come to dominate human life. Perhaps the imaginative power of the human mind is sometimes too powerful for its own good; perhaps it's the price we pay for our intelligence. Fear can take us over, narrowing the scope of our lives and persuading us too often to choose the security of a familiar world rather than the adventure of growth and new experience.

People can be afraid of all kinds of things, some rational, some deeply irrational. Some people are afraid of death, perhaps because it is so unknowable in advance, and perhaps because it means the definitive end of this magical experience of life. Other people fear not coping, or depression, or going mad. All of these are in some degree universal human instincts, perhaps in normal conditions an acceptable part of the picture, but potentially disabling if allowed to grow out of a natural proportion.

Perhaps the one fear underlying all others is the fear of not making any sense at all. Dying maybe isn't so bad in itself; the ultimate fear might be expressed in the prayer, 'Lord, I know I must die, but let me not perish!' To perish might be to die in confusion, having failed to understand what life was all about, to die with neither meaning nor dignity nor worth. And meaning isn't just about finding intellectually satisfying answers. Life has meaning when we have confidence in our own worth, either because someone loves us or because we have come to understand that we are special, children of a generous creation, precious in the eyes of our creator. In the end, perhaps, all of these can feel very much like the same thing.

Life is a huge puzzle which we have to figure out as we experience it, and we are made to get to the bottom of puzzles. Human beings thrive and prosper when they find a belief in themselves, often through finding a role, sometimes in a family or relationship, sometimes in employment or among friends and acquaintances. So much human dysfunction and misery arises when people cannot find anything to love or believe in within themselves, and when this happens fear can run out of control, making a hell out of a potential heaven.

On this theme again Jesus does seem to be saying something of immediate interest to human beings in any age. This is the human sickness he is so keen to understand, and his prescription can transform our understanding of ourselves, and our journey, and the rest of our lives, if we choose to take it.

Chapter 9
Diagnosing the Heart

The Dynamics of Human Imperfection

The word 'sin' can still get a strong negative reaction from people today. Many people are simply allergic to it. Over the centuries, churches have badly overplayed the themes of sin and guilt, some say, and now many people feel indignant that they have been oppressed for so long in this way. We have inherited a dark, pessimistic image of human nature which seems a world away from Jesus' own teaching.

It does seem odd to say this, though. The twentieth century has possibly seen more human-inflicted evil than any previous era, on a worldwide scale, culminating in horrors like Auschwitz, Dresden and Hiroshima. Seen in the light of all this, the idea that there is a basic kink in human nature, some kind of internal contradiction, seems to have a certain plausibility to it. Indeed perhaps it's our very resistance to the idea which seems suspicious.

Significantly it is often women theologians who have turned around our way of seeing the subject of sin in our own times. Power-based systems have, not surprisingly, laid stress on the sin of pride and the need for humility, and have become perhaps unduly preoccupied with sexuality; this has produced a needlessly tortured idea of human nature which women have found especially oppressive. Originally the word 'sin' simply indicated a falling short of a standard, without the deadweight of unworthiness which became attached to it later.

One modern author, Dorin Barter, attempts to redefine the word like this: 'The emphasis has shifted from sinful acts to the experience we have of a disturbed or damaged relationship with God – towards goodness, reality or authenticity.' For the standard which we fall short of she coins the term 'livingness', and she comments that 'reality is the very central rightness of life … it feeds the livingness which makes life gracious and strong'. She then goes on to conclude that 'sin steals livingness from us when we are its victims, it blocks reality from us when we are sinners'. [53] So sin damages our sense of reality and our experience of the fullness of life.

It was Mother Julian of Norwich who realized that sin was part of the glory of how we are created, part of the logic and the dynamic of human experience. First we fall, and the pain is real, but then we see ourselves more clearly. It's almost as if we need to sin, stumble and fall in order to see ourselves in perspective. Our creator, moreover, has made us this way and therefore doesn't condemn us – on the contrary, the pain of living is always surrounded by his (or her) enthusiastic love for us.[54]

Are we not strange as well as glorious creatures, falling for one addictive pleasure after another yet also capable of catching the awesome beauty of our surrounding creation, stumbling and transcending, sinning and worshipping – often within the same quarter of an hour! Many of us can recognize the positively bizarre experience of seeking happiness from a source which we know perfectly well will not satisfy us, and then suffering the inevitable disappointment. Logic seemingly isn't enough to convince us; we need to go through the hard route of experience to learn better, and sometimes even this isn't enough to really teach us. This was caught by the creator of the Charlie Brown cartoon some years ago, when he entitled one of his stories 'The wages of sin is "Aauugghhh!"' (Was the book called *The Gospel according to Peanuts*?)

Through all this we can recognize an inner dynamic at work, whole systems of defense within us which spring into action to protect us from anything which seems to threaten our comfort. The story related in Genesis chapter 2 highlights one of these human defense mechanisms especially clearly when Adam says,

Don't look at me – it was that woman who started it. And Eve (significantly protecting Adam) points at the snake! We're still at it today, projecting blame on anyone or anything but ourselves. Somewhere inside, there is a mechanism which springs to our defense and in the process, ironically, often blinds us to a wider truth.

Another defense mechanism is simply to repress, to send down into oblivion anything too threatening or painful for us to bear. This is certainly more tender territory, all of us in some degree needing this mechanism of selective forgetting to function as normal adults. It can be a real blessing that our brains censor out much of the unpleasant side of our experience, especially some of the memories from childhood, when our self-confidence was still fragile, our personality still in the process of forming.

In another mechanism our unconscious preselects what we notice and remember in all kinds of situations. Two people can walk down the same street at the same moment and see entirely different things. Let's say one is running late to an appointment with the bank manager and doesn't notice the band playing on the corner, while the other stops to enjoy the music and happens to notice one young woman... You know the story. What we see or hear depends on what we have been set up to see or hear.

These preselective mechanisms can of course also work the other way, selecting too much. For example, if there is something maybe a bit tender which we don't wish to think about, they can give us a narrow, unrealistic picture of our reality, screening off too much from us. Some of us have an unreasonably modest or even negative picture of ourselves; others survive on a saccharine-sweet fable. How many of us recognize something like this within ourselves?

It does begin to look as if we wouldn't be able to function at all without a chorus of mechanisms continuously working away inside us, in their own way looking after our welfare, or our interests, or some of the time our whims. Is this the reason why we sometimes go to so much trouble to avoid the very thing which will give us deepest satisfaction, preferring instead to stick to other routines and habits which are maybe second-rate and keep us tied down but have the benefit of being more familiar and comforting? And is this why we sometimes recognize yet resist the appeal of this new vision of Jesus' inner Kingdom, with its promise of more creative, abundant living? Has the experience of living made us more cautious than is good for us, maybe knocking the taste for this kind of adventure right out of us?

Judgment Day!

Another good illustration of the peculiar dynamics at play within us in everyday living is when we respond to a sense of guilt. Of course the topic of guilt, like sin, has been badly overplayed by the churches, and many people are still angry about this. But we do all know what it is to feel guilty about something, do we not? We can all recognize situations, for example, in which we have hurt or insulted someone, perhaps in a rapid exchange of angry words, or perhaps unintentionally in a moment of slack thinking. Two things are perhaps worth noticing in these situations. First, there is often a very stubborn resistance within us to any idea of apologizing or making a gesture of reconciliation. Second, if we ever do manage to admit openly that we may have been wrong and our gesture of reconciliation is accepted, there is often a sense of liberation from a burden which has been weighing us down. It can be like witnessing to a truth within us.

The four Gospel narratives do record times when Jesus showed a flashing anger, but vengeful punishment is somehow alien to the spirit of his teaching. He does speak of a day of judgment, and this is tied up with his ideas about the end-time when wrongs would be righted and tears finally wiped away. But what are we to make of the idea of judgment today? Where does it find echoes in our experience and in our unconscious?

The Kingdom teaching is partly about facing truth and the frequent difficulty of doing so, battling against these so-called defense mechanisms within us. But maybe the idea of being judged in the light of this truth needn't be as threatening as it seems. For one thing, truth is balanced, and any true verdict will give credit for the good we have done, something which may come as something of a pleasant surprise to us! Perhaps more important, when we are faced with the weaknesses and inadequacies we all of us have, although at first this can be an uncomfortable or even frightening experience, it can often turn out better than we had feared. Although it may have to cause us pain at the time, like some medical treatment, maybe it will end up doing us more good than we would have thought.

Jesus' Kingdom teaching can make a difference because it can give us a reason to pluck up courage and face our fear. Even in a worst-case scenario, even when we do deserve condemnation over something, this condemnation is never going to be final or dismissive. On the contrary it can be deeply creative and can lead to personal renewal and new beginnings, because it is set within the overwhelming generosity of our creation. We are held by an energy – a love, if you will – which is simply not capable of abandoning us since it is part of how we are created. So being judged, or facing the unacceptable side of ourselves, may turn out to be a part of our completion, like a homecoming to our full humanity. For quite a lot of people, though, this judgment can be hard to accept. Some have a morbid, overdeveloped sense of unworthiness which is quite out of proportion to their actual deserts.

Others again, sadly, may have done so much damage to themselves or others around them that they find it impossible to face the excruciating truth about their guilt, protecting themselves instead with webs of fantasy, excuse and denial. Perhaps one of the worst consequences of doing evil things is that it can truly exile the perpetrator from reality, as Dorin Barter saw, robbing them of access to a crucial part of their humanity. Facing this kind of truth can sometimes take a lifetime; indeed it is often triggered by some trauma, like a bereavement. Sometimes the sense of being forgiven despite everything can give people the courage to confront their reality. But many individuals never ever make this breakthrough into the real world – a paralyzing fear keeps them imprisoned. Judgment can be awesome, harsh and yet cleansing for those who finally face it, but it can seem a whole lot more menacing for those who never manage to face it.

Truth does matter to us, yet we spend so much energy trying to disguise it or escape from it. Jesus' Kingdom teaching crucially introduces the idea of an internal agent, a kind of Angel of Truth working on our side within us. Perhaps the work of this agent within us has something to do with sorting out this jungle of edgy defense mechanisms, calming their fears and gradually taking charge on behalf of us and on behalf of the truth within us. Judgment Day, then, is part of the idea of the Kingdom of Heaven within us and the continuous action of this Angel of Truth, alias Holy Spirit, this internal advocate witnessing to truth within us despite the lies and half-truths and evasions which our defense mechanisms so often feed us with.

So Judgment Day isn't some red-letter day in the future. This court session doesn't convene after we die; it's timeless. It's more like a court sitting continuously within every human heart. Truth can be frightening, like a cleansing flame which (as they say) hurts like hell at the time, which is why we run away from it. But in the end, if we can summon the courage to face it, this court is perhaps more like a tribunal than a criminal court. Its aim is not so much to send us down in flames, but to get at the truth.

A New Courage
Jesus urges us to love our enemies, to do good even to those who wish to harm us. In modern times, strangely, this is sometimes

understood to be a soft, passive option. In practice his recommended responses to oppression, for example, seem to be non-violent but very challenging, requiring a good deal of courage. This is memorably set out by Walter Wink, who projects an entirely new light on three examples of Jesus' teaching.[55] Incidentally, these illustrate very graphically how we have lost the cultural context of a story over the passing centuries, causing us to significantly misunderstand its original point.

For example, 'If someone in authority presses you into service for one mile, go with him two.' We think we understand what this is saying here – the phrase 'going the extra mile' is after all embedded in our language – but the original meaning adds quite another dimension. Under Roman military regulations a soldier or official was entitled to commandeer help in carrying what were often substantial loads of equipment and supplies, but only for one mile. The point about offering to go an extra mile is that this would be against regulations. By doing this you'd therefore be inviting this soldier to break the law and put himself in danger, reminding him of the injustice of his original command. This is resistance, not generosity. It is sophisticated non-violent action, a way of calmly asserting your own dignity in the face of potential violence, recalling modern tactics of non-violent resistance in the way that it appeals directly to the humanity of the man behind the uniform.

Likewise, 'If anyone takes your coat, let him have your shirt as well.' Again this is not some whimsical generosity. By offering to take off your shirt, your undergarment, you are threatening to strip naked in front of your challenger! In the culture of the time, nakedness was a source of shame more for the observer than for the naked person. So again this course of action is designed to stop this person in his tracks and make him ashamed, reminding him of the injustice of his action.

The third example is probably the most famous and perhaps the most misunderstood of the three: 'If someone strikes you on the right cheek, turn and offer him the other as well.' A blow to the right cheek was a backhand blow which was given by a master to his servant or by a solder to a peasant. It was an assertion of social superiority and the power that goes with it. For the victim then to offer his left cheek was to invite a blow with the closed fist, which in that culture was only used in combat between equals. To offer the left cheek was therefore to refuse to accept a second backhand blow and to assert your equality with the aggressor.

This kind of resistance against an overwhelmingly more powerful adversary is in fact so sophisticated that it looks as if it may have been part of a conscious counterculture. These three examples sound like tried-and-tested, very deliberate strategies, and the fact that Jesus advocates them seems to hint at an early time of contact with some kind of national resistance subculture.

Where does the courage for this non-violent resistance come from? It can come from a sense of dignity arising from a new status as members of this new Kingdom, inspiring us to hold our head up, to see through the violence and to even show a compassionate respect to our adversary. Quite apart from anything else, this kind of courage is bound to attract the thoughtful admiration of others. It was exactly this kind of Christian courage in the face of fearsome persecution which later attracted significant numbers of early converts to this growing new faith.

Jesus is talking about nothing less than the liberation of the human spirit, a liberation which can truly move mountains, bringing the miracle of courage to the fearful and compassion to the bitterest of hearts, a compassion which can reach out even to your persecutor.

Chapter 10
Homage

This Timeless Kingdom

At this point maybe it's worth dwelling for a moment on the simply extraordinary idea of a Kingdom within the heart. At first sight this is surely an unlikely metaphor, creating a whole other reality, an alternative universe of love and truth inside us which binds us all together. It also creates a new kind of authority, an authority which wins our willing allegiance and to which we submit out of admiration and love rather than out of fear. This remarkable new reality in turn teaches us a new self-respect and opens up a whole new future for us.

For Jesus to take a political, public concept – a Kingdom – and use it to, in effect, invent a new reality within the heart is a truly extraordinary leap of the imagination. Today we might compare it with the greatest of modern fiction in its ability to help us see new worlds, new dimensions in ourselves. But then we remember that Jesus' whole style of teaching did, after all, involve telling stories from life in order to throw light on deeper internal truths. At heart he was an instinctive storyteller, and that perhaps is why he could see new realities quite beyond the limits of conventional reason.

Some people object to the idea of a Kingdom because it seems to imply a king who is liable to boss us around and rob us of our freedom. For this reason the writer Philip Pullman refers instead to a Republic of Heaven (borrowing in turn from the English radical Gerrard Winstanley), and in a sense he is quite right. Confusingly, Jesus does seem to mix his metaphors. But although he calls this inner reality a Kingdom, he thinks of his God not really as a king but crucially as a parent, an image which fits the intimate inner world much more naturally. (This mixed metaphor, incidentally, could be a vivid unconscious witness to a vision in the very process of being shaped – minted new – bringing together two quite separate influences on him: the political struggle against the Romans, and his own experience of family life.)

Meanwhile the word 'Kingdom' has taken on new life. Today we use it to refer to realms of the natural world, like the invertebrate kingdom or the kingdom of trees and plants. This sense of the word has of course no king, no human-like authority, but it does have patterns or regularities which we sometimes refer to as laws – another non-scientific metaphor borrowed from elsewhere. Jesus' new inner Kingdom, too, although it doesn't have a king in any literal sense, does imply something like law, some force born in us to which we instinctively turn. This is an authority within us which we habitually disobey and yet come home to, which at some level we acknowledge and yet for long periods ignore, which we struggle against and yet fly to. It has no power in the social or political sense, but it has the power of truth and love which is greater than any other human power, in the end because it is built into our very nature.

The Logic of Hyperbole

As the early Christian centuries wore on, the hyperbole surrounding the cult of Jesus began to create wholly new strands of logical reasoning. If he was the savior of the world, then he had obviously been a wonder child who could foretell his own future. But this was only the start. Once people had concluded that he was actually a pre-existent constituent of the creator, then a veritable torrent of attributes had to follow. So Jesus in time becomes omniscient, omnipotent, sinless, and acquires a host of other attributes like physical beauty, in the end becoming the recipient of every perfection anyone could ever think of. All of this renders him more and more unreal and makes his intimate vision of his Abba more and more distant from ordinary folk. He has become unreachable, and this in effect nullifies the whole point of his teaching.

Fortunately this kind of logic carries little appeal today. Nevertheless quite a lot of this hyperbole from past ages still hangs around in our minds. If Jesus is sinless, this soon begins to mean that he never made mistakes, was always right and never said a word out of place. Comparing him even to the likes of Shakespeare can be met in some religious quarters with disbelief or even laughter. In theory, church doctrine insists on Jesus' full humanity, but in practice the culture of the churches so often still undermines this.

For example, our understanding of sexuality has changed in quite fundamental ways, and so the traditional idea that he was somehow above sexual experience – an idea influenced by many centuries of despising the body and confusing sex with sin and depravity – will surely no longer do. Sexuality is now seen as centrally and quintessentially human, and if we are to see Jesus in his full humanity we need perhaps to restore an everyday sexual dimension to the picture. This can throw a new light onto many accounts of his interaction with other people. For example, in his encounter with the woman who bathed his feet in her tears, recounted in Chapter 3, his compassion can now become once again the normal compassion you would expect of a young man for a woman in distress.

The writer of the letter to the Hebrews says that Jesus had 'learned obedience through his sufferings'[56]. Jesus' very evident empathy for suffering in other people, indeed his calling to become a healer, were no doubt built on early foundations. His long meditation on the meaning of suffering and on the healing of human nature surely arose from his own experience of the hammer blows he had gone through himself. There is just a hint from those who knew him that his early years may have been marked by sorrow.

The Achievement

Jesus' vision is steeped in Jewish writings and tradition. Many of his ideas have been taken from prophets like Second Isaiah and Daniel, and many others reflect streams within the political liberation thinking of his time. There again, quite a number of Jesus' sayings bear striking resemblance to sayings of other Jewish teachers of the time, like Rabbi Hillel, one of the founders of early modern Judaism.

Yet it does seem that during the short period of his teaching described in the four Gospels, his understanding goes through a transformation. John Robinson discerns the possibility of three phases in this deepening of Jesus' vision.[57] First, Jesus associated himself with the call to repentance and national renewal which John the Baptist preached, and with it the arrival of a powerful messiah. After the desert temptations, new themes are heard, of personal healing, the elixir of life – the pearl of great price, as he called it – and the special role of the outcasts and those who suffer. Later still, the theme of suffering is extended back to his own role, with the old prophetic idea of a suffering servant, and of victory through what appeared to be defeat.

In this process the Kingdom of Heaven has gone from a public, political aspiration to an internal reality within us all, and the God of Israel has become the intimate presence of Abba in the heart. These are enormous changes. This is a distinctive kind of genius who can see new realities within familiar traditional themes. Jesus assembles a number of ideas familiar at the time and then gives them a uniquely different understanding which transforms the significance of the whole vision.

He teaches in a tradition of wisdom teachers, through stories from life and through memorable aphorisms. He is a master of words, for example in the Jewish tradition of debate. The Gospels relate examples when he checkmates his opponents by asking them questions which they cannot answer either way without losing face or getting themselves into deeper water. But he also is wary of words; he understands their limits, and supplements them periodically by a series of dramatic public actions, like overturning the tables of the money changers in the great temple, or entering Jerusalem on the back of a donkey. He often uses words sparingly and understands that actions reach people much more effectively. His reaction to Zacchaeus (outlined in Chapter 6) is a good example of this, and his acts of healing can be seen, too, as part of this pattern, evidence of this recurring impatience with words. It goes without saying that the crucifixion fits into the same pattern. Add all this together and the magnetism of his charismatic presence is clear – there are several occasions in the Gospel records where people give up jobs or families in order to follow him. And all this in a man probably in his early thirties.

What is new in Jesus' teaching may be in part a reflection of the wider cultural influences to which Jewish society was exposed by his time. The small province of Galilee in particular contained several major Greek towns, one of them, Sepphoris, only a few miles from the village of Nazareth. Attempts to reconcile the Jewish tradition with Greek thought were a feature of the times. So perhaps not surprisingly, people have noticed points of similarity in Jesus' teaching with other non-Jewish thinkers of his time. Wandering teachers called Cynics (no relation to the modern meaning of the word) taught a sober skepticism about the delusions of materialism, and preached a withdrawal into an inner life. Another school, the Stoics, are remembered for their determination to follow justice and virtue, and for their calm and courageous acceptance of fate. Plato, and even more his later followers, exerted a considerable influence on classical church theology at a critical stage in its development. There are points of comparison with Jesus' thinking in all of these. But Jesus is nevertheless unique among these schools of thought in a number of ways.

Jesus' teaching handles the ubiquity and the key importance

of paradox in understanding the complex dynamics of human nature. He understands not only the inherent limits of words but also the dynamic, many-layered nature of the mind, with its temptations and resistance mechanisms which create the essential drama of human life. Long before the discovery of the unconscious, he sees the contradictory yearnings within the heart, its essential dilemma and the difficulty of seeing a way out unaided. His teaching includes a critique of society, human competitiveness, hierarchies and the limits of politics. It sees right through the conventional surface of life into a new vision of humanity set within the framework of the creation itself, a vision which can transform the meaning and the quality of the experience of life for every one of us. Taken together this is extraordinary in its reach.

This new vision of the inner Kingdom of Heaven mirrors the heart in its unpredictable, mysteriously creative, anarchic quality, so diametrically opposite in nature to political or organizational hierarchies and rule books. His understanding of the similarity of the spirit of childhood to this inner Kingdom perhaps finds a very special echo today. In modern times we understand that the child we once were throws a long shadow into our adult lives, and many modern adults remember and occasionally yearn for a lost magic. Jesus says the spirit of his Kingdom is like the spirit of childhood. It's as if he is telling us that something of this lost magic can return to us and transform us.

In other ways his teaching is a manifesto of hope and defiance against the odds of fate. He sees the central importance of the outcasts, those whom fate has hit hardest, people on the edge of life who were scorned or barely noticed by the rest. It's the powerless and those who suffer who can see the vision of the living God as no one else does, he says. This is social dynamite, giving an entirely new source of respect to the ranks of the socially despised. He sees the soporific effect of privilege and power and money, blinding people to their more fundamental needs, and likewise the oddly paradoxical blessing which can come with adversity, bringing us up sharp to our ultimate realities. This kind of insight is both subtle and searching. Both in his time and for many centuries thereafter, he really has few equals in the depth and the dynamism of his thinking about humanity and its needs.

But all this still leaves out what is perhaps his main achievement: the way in which he opens up a whole new emotional language for us. For Jesus, the work of his Abba within each of us is a loving and confirming, a healing and liberating work, firing us with a new energy and self-belief. Today we know that our species is unique in the open-ended, unfinished nature of our minds. Emotionally we need to complete ourselves through learning and experience, more than any other species. The vision of this Kingdom permits us to see the possibility of humanity trans-formed, of its latent, potential at last released, creating an exhila-rating experience of life with an intoxicating quality.

This is the thinking of a shamanic or prophetic tradition. We can recognize its truth not principally by the exercise of surface reasoning but more essentially at a level deep underneath the workings of the conscious mind. An appeal to reason may not take us very far, it seems; perhaps only an appeal to the depths of the human heart may yet manage to turn us around. Jesus' thinking anticipates the unconscious.

This remarkable visionary dares us to take a leap of trust which truly can dispel the nagging fears of the heart, even that ultimate shadow: the fear of death itself. Who else can make such compelling sense of such an impossibly contrary and illogical mass of emotions and yearnings? The Jewish writer Geza Vermes describes Jesus as 'second to none in profundity of insight and grandeur of character', and as 'an unsurpassed master of the art of laying bare the inmost core of spiritual truth'.[58] This Jesus, this ambassador of the inner Kingdom, stands comparison with anyone.

Part Three
This is the Man

The two chapters of Part Three together form a long meditation on the events of the passion narratives, assessing different ways in which these sensational developments were interpreted by different witnesses. Crucially, this meditation tries to find a logic linking these events back to Jesus' earlier teaching about the Kingdom of Heaven within us.

In teasing apart an often enigmatic mass of detail in the evidence, it treats perhaps overheated theorizing and speculation with a certain caution. It also tries to understand how some of Jesus' followers might have understood these events at the time, and finally wonders how Jesus himself might have responded to it all.

Chapter 11
The Passion Narratives

Throughout the Bible, narrative tends to illustrate theology; facts follow meaning, not the other way round. Again and again the narratives are chosen for inclusion in the text because they illustrate some meaning; otherwise they would have been left out. Certainly the four accounts of the passion story are written to demonstrate the meaning which Jesus had for their various writers. Indeed they differ in the detail they bring out precisely because their understanding of the underlying meaning of it all differs in detail from one to another. There is an unconscious honesty to all this. These narratives are full of compelling human detail, yet in places they also hesitate about the parts of the story they are *not* sure of; in fact they are content to reveal a whole knot of ambiguities within it. All four Gospel narratives strain to find a logic linking their two major themes: the passion events and the Kingdom teaching which had preceded them. There is a degree of uncertainty about their accounts, and they are content to reflect this in the text.

For example, one common traditional defense of belief in the resurrection is that after the crucifixion Jesus had appeared to his followers and that that had quite simply settled it. But the narratives relate that Jesus had appeared only to really quite a limited number of followers. How were all the others supposed to believe their reports? The record, indeed, tells us frankly that some followers didn't believe them at all.[59]

The idea that reports of Jesus' appearances were self-authenticating not only underrates the mystery surrounding the events themselves. It also tends to skip over the severity of the trauma which the followers had just been through. Perhaps above all, though, it underrates the strong thematic links which presumably there must be between the two themes, the two stages of the story. Had there been no significant links between Jesus' Kingdom teaching and the events of the passion, this would make of the whole thing not just a mystery but something close to a nonsense. The presumption has to be that the passion events in some way fulfilled the teaching, if the thing is to make any sense at all.

What Happened? And What Did it Mean?

On one level Jesus died because in the eyes of the provincial Roman authorities he appeared to be challenging their power at the most volatile, dangerous time in the Jewish year. Jerusalem was full of pilgrims and there was a constant danger of riot. The Romans thought he might just cause them trouble, and their usual, brutal rule of thumb was: If in doubt, execute. Jewish authorities followed a different logic. It is better, they reasoned, that one man should die for the people, than that the whole nation be destroyed by the fury of the Roman power. Ironically they were in their own way absolutely right. In the following century a whole series of revolts did indeed induce a Roman response of such escalating ferocity that eventually it did in a sense destroy the whole nation.

Did Jesus have a choice in doing what he did? Could he have gone back to Galilee and carried on teaching and healing? He himself apparently didn't think so. He does seem to have believed that he had to confront Roman power openly, in the belief that somehow he would be vindicated. So in the end he caught the attention of the authorities by causing a fracas in the temple complex of all places, and then relied on the rumor mill to do the rest. By now we can recognize that this sometimes intemperate young man knew what he was doing and what consequences were liable to follow. The casual murder of his kinsman and former mentor John at the court of a local prince must have made a lasting impression on him. Independent records tell us that the Romans on occasion crucified by the thousands, and it is unlikely that Jesus did not know about this. It seems to have been a calculated, highly courageous challenge.

The public destruction of this highly charismatic teacher of the secret of life was evidently catastrophic to his followers. Today we forget just how savage this destruction was intended to be. In a deeply religious age it was an important part of the punishment to refuse the rites of burial and this meant quite simply leaving the victim to the crows and the jackals. Roman logic was mercilessly brutal. The process was designed to crush the will of the followers, and at first, it seems, it did exactly that.

To the followers this savage turn of events appeared to annul every word Jesus had said. To use his own terms, it seemed after all like a definitive victory of the kingdoms of this world over the Kingdom of Heaven. The words from the cross in Mark's account have a candid ring about them: 'My God, my God, why have you forsaken me?[60]' The public humiliation would have mattered. The soldiers, we are told, shared out his clothes amongst themselves.[61] There is no mention of the loincloth which spares his dignity in the pictures and models of him made after the passing of many centuries. Back then, victims were helplessly naked in public as their bodily excretions trickled down the wood, all part of a fierce and deliberate public humiliation. The traumatic impact on the few who had had the courage to follow and observe this from a distance must have been severe, and doubly so for the few brave souls who dared to come closer.

After the unforgettable months of elation and growing certainty, it had all come down to this. Shockingly, in the eyes of Jesus' followers, God had not rescued him, and the idea that God could behave like that to his chosen messiah simply strained belief. Perhaps Jesus hadn't been the prophet of God they all took him to be. For them, the God of Israel doesn't abandon his chosen messenger like that. Many of those who had understood Jesus' teaching as principally about political liberation must have had their hopes dashed beyond recovery.

For those, however, who had seen that this teaching was about a Kingdom not of this world, other thoughts would come to the surface sooner or later. They would remember that Jesus had gone out of his way to challenge the public power of the Romans. The thought would eventually come to them that if Jesus' Kingdom was truly not of this world then physical execution would not be able to touch it. This apparent destruction might then strangely turn out to be a victory, only at first people were blind to it until it was given to them to see it later, suddenly, in a rush of euphoric relief.

This conclusion was so very strange that understandably it may have taken some time before it really caught on with a wider circle of followers, but when it did they expressed this new conviction in the way most natural for them: Jesus had returned from the land of the dead. The rumors that he was alive must be true. The Kingdom of Heaven would prevail over the kingdoms of this world after all.

Jesus' had apparently challenged the Roman public authority, the very epitome of the kingdoms of this world, in the faith that the inner Kingdom of the heart would in the end be seen to be indestructible. His followers had no idea how to explain this, but they believed it because it tied everything together, because everything made sense again. As they saw it, the blessing of the Kingdom had come flooding back to them, even across the barrier of death itself.

The dawning of a new light of understanding in the minds of the followers is told in one of the great passages of the narrative Gospels, positively hair-raising in its psychological acuity: the story of the journey to Emmaus.[62] Two followers are trudging their way home from Jerusalem evidently in deep shock; a stranger joins them on the way and they fall into a long discussion. Significantly, these followers are dismayed at the execution of the man they had hoped would liberate Israel –

again, people still seeing him as a political figure. When they reach home he makes as if to carry on the journey but they invite him in to eat with them, still suspecting nothing. Then he raises his hands to bless the meal. Is there something about the way he does this, some habitual personal mannerism in the way he performs this homely ritual? Suddenly they recognize him.

The story says that at this point he vanishes from their sight, but crucially it is when they remember his words that the light really dawns. 'Were not our hearts on fire as he talked with us on the road?' they recall. He had told them that these shocking events had had to be; they had been necessary in order to fulfill God's purposes, purposes already discerned by prophets in the past about the saving of the nations.

Still, the resurrection stories in the four narratives again and again come back to a sense of uncertainty and ambiguity. On more than one occasion people don't recognize Jesus at first. In some stories he is present in a very physical way, for example asking if they have any food; in others he appears suddenly, sometimes comes through locked doors, and just as suddenly vanishes. This uncertainty is plausible, given the state of confusion and grief amongst his followers. Short of actual hallucinations, grief over someone who has been greatly loved can produce a deeply consoling sense of their continuing presence.

In the midst of all this, it's the remembered teaching about new life and the victory of the Kingdom over death that convinces them in the end. And the energy of the new faith is the energy of people suddenly released from an unbearable ambiguity, first into a period of incredulous doubt and hesitation, and finally into a new explosive joy and clarity of understanding. Psychologically this rings true, does it not? Often the strongest beliefs come when a really distressing uncertainty is eventually resolved. The earliest origins of Christianity, then, are rooted in the experience of people who have just survived major trauma. The followers, too, have been through a living death and have come back to life.

Chasing the Enigma

Some of the followers, then, united around the sensational belief that their beloved teacher had risen from the dead. But this still left the question why it had been necessary for him to go through all this in the first place. Evidently those around him had been, in any case, in some difficulty trying to make sense of this enigmatic, compelling teaching, and various attempts to explain the mystery were put forward. How do these attempts match up with the remembered teaching?

Did Jesus die for us? In one sense perhaps yes. The fear of death nags at the back of all our minds, a universal symptom of the human condition. Here was trust in his Abba right through death itself. The thing is, Jesus never just theorized. Teaching and actions had to be a seamless whole: he healed the sick, he challenged the kingdoms of this world, he trusted through death. It's part of the whole vision. An older man might have contented himself with teaching, and lived a long life. But this young man was fired with the heat of his vision, giving him an uncompromising, heady kind of courage. And this vision was so ravishing, so intoxicating. This relationship of utter trust was the pearl of great price he had spoken of. In the end it does seem to have been the fire of this vision which gave him the physical courage to take on the kingdoms of this world head-on. This, then, was no reckless, despairing suicide. This was done in the conviction that he would be vindicated, although he may not have been certain in detail how this would come about.

Did he die for us? In another sense perhaps not. If his death was necessary to cleanse us from our sins, or to pay a ransom for us to an august, righteous God, this would seem to cut across the whole spirit of his teaching. This view of the atonement doctrine as a punishment accepted by Jesus on our behalf recalls the ancient Jewish theme of the scapegoat, an animal ritually made to carry the sins and misdemeanors of the tribe, and driven out into the desert. But this way of understanding God doesn't really match Jesus' own vision of Abba, whose love and generosity floods over us every moment. The human condition was like a sickness; it was compared to a blindness or an inability to walk, something incomplete in us which kept us in exile from the overwhelming, unconditional love of our creator. Healing was the constant motif of the Gospels, not punishment, least of all a punishment required in order to expunge some cosmic evil deep-set into human nature. This sounds more like a quid pro quo, canceling a debt of honor, something surely more reminiscent of the iron law of the vendetta.

The idea that sin required a death, a sacrifice, was certainly familiar to Jews and pagans alike in that era, and that no doubt is one reason why writers grasped at it to explain the apparent contradiction and shock of Jesus' death. The idea that it was necessary for him to take due punishment on our behalf certainly can move people, but it does encourage us to talk up our incorrigible unworthiness and perpetual guilt in order to magnify this dramatic act of saving us from our supposed true deserts. It fits awkwardly with the message of healing, homecoming and celebration of the overwhelming generosity of our creator and of his ever-present closeness in our inner Kingdom. Doesn't this punitive way of thinking look backwards at the very mindset which Jesus' extraordinary vision had overturned?

More recent thinking on the atonement doctrine, however, links it at a level deep within us to a power which can heal all that is alien and fragmented in us, body and soul, female and male, sexual and spiritual, nature and humanity. How can it do this? Often it takes tragedy to move people out of habitual ruts, a theme taken up many times in fiction and drama. Very often, argument on its own will not move us, but the suffering and death of a loved one can do so. People, moreover, so often go through their lives without the public permission to mourn the devastating blows which their own experience has dealt out to them. Then someone else, perhaps someone famous or greatly respected, dies, and suddenly there is permission to break through their inhibitions and let out their long pent-up grief in public. Perhaps this can give a new meaning to the biblical text 'Surely he hath borne *our* griefs, and carried *our* sorrows'? [63]

There is a deep emotional logic here which can move us at a level far beneath rational argument.

At some point Jesus, it seems, came to see that words on their own might not move people enough to change their entire way of living. Perhaps only the enactment of this teaching in a dramatic act of self-giving would have the emotional power to really reach people, would permit people to pour out their own accumulated grief of living and finally allow them to change. Perhaps atonement can be understood afresh after all, as a ritual myth embodying Jesus' central theme of love healing the brokenness in the human heart. And perhaps the emotional release which it can give us really can change us because it gives us the sense that we have at last been understood. Our outpouring of grief is, in short, cathartic. We feel renewed. These are deep waters.

But while this extraordinarily dramatic, oddly powerful story can move us today, there is no denying that it can still come across to many of us as very strange. Culturally it is maybe just too far removed from us. So perhaps Jesus today, across the barriers separating alien cultures, just leaves us with an oddly compelling, open-ended mystery. Perhaps Jesus experienced a sense of mystery in this too – we get from him a sense of trusting through uncertainty, even when it was not given to him to understand in detail exactly what he had to go through. In the end his teaching leaves us too with a sense of the overarching mystery of our existence, of life and death alike.

Certainly, the seemingly deliberate nature of his death can cause problems for us today, as indeed it did for early Christians too. In time it became a model for others during ferocious persecution and fanned the hysteria of a cult of martyrdom. This has undoubtedly colored all later images of Jesus, making him seem half in love with death for its own sake, and this in turn has fed the idea that this world was nothing, nothing but a preparation for a better world to come. But Jesus keeps saying that the Kingdom starts in the present tense; it has already arrived, and this is cause for great celebration right now. The Gospel record portrays him as a man with a zest for this life here and now, a man with an affectionate compassion for people, a quick, observant sense of humor and an enjoyment of good company.

The truth is that, for Jesus, life and death were in practical terms probably not opposites at all. Part of the key to opening up to life's full potential, strange to say, was to accept the need for the kind of trusting acceptance involved in dying. Letting go of ego, 'dying' to our neurotic need to control everything and have everything – this was perhaps the key to the whole thing. Jesus' insight has been compared to that of some of the Greek philosophers, or indeed to that of some eastern religions. Once you have found this key to the secret of life, the puzzling prospect of death loses the menacing temporal finality it once had. Its sting has been drawn. Once you have been freed to love with all your mind and all your soul and all your strength, once the ecstasy of this love has fired you, life is no longer temporally bound. It becomes eternal, free of the underlying anxieties and limits of time.

Some Christian people still insist on the need to believe in a physical resurrection. Paul is often quoted: 'If Christ was not raised from the dead, then our gospel is null and void ... [and] we of all people are most to be pitied.'[64] Here Paul, like Thomas before him, seems to need his proof, some reassurance that Jesus had indeed prevailed. Others argue that the resurrection Paul is primarily interested in is resurrection within the human heart. But today it's not instantly clear how one man's return from the grave gives rise to this resurrection within the heart and thus saves the rest of us. This logic, once presumably clear to people of another time, has become pretty obscure to many in our own day.

This insistence on a literal view, consciously inspired by Paul's words, gets to the heart of the credibility problem mentioned earlier in this book. It is, after all, no more than reasonable for open-minded, sympathetic people in our own time to doubt the possibility of a literal resurrection from the dead. For most of us, our world simply doesn't work that way. Perhaps Christianity deserves broader, more convincing foundations than these strangely arbitrary, not to say perilously slender ones. Fortunately, the logic of another great New Testament thinker, the author of the fourth Gospel, can speak to us perhaps more directly today. Jesus' teaching can convince us because it speaks directly to the heart, reflecting that light which is in us from birth. This vision of the Kingdom stands on its own, requiring no further miracles to prove it.

To put it bluntly, most people today would quite naturally say, 'Well, if Jesus was alive after the crucifixion, he can't have been properly dead before it.' Today we would naturally talk of survival rather than resurrection, and for us this really is a matter of definition, not evidence. But there was another side to how people saw things then. A text from the Psalms was used by Peter in his oration to the crowd at Pentecost:

For you will not abandon me to death,
nor let your faithful servant suffer corruption.[65]

Evidently some early Christians had come to the conclusion that although Jesus had died, God had at that point intervened after all. He had not allowed him to 'see corruption'. In the logic of their own times, Jesus was taken through death and brought back out again. In modern logic this might be taken to mean that he had gone near to that irreversible point where 'corruption' sets in, but had been brought back to consciousness before reaching it. It's the definition of death which has changed.

In fact the whole story of the passion events in the four New Testament narratives is laced through and through with mystery and ambiguity. For example, the Roman legate Pontius Pilate clearly had had some trouble coming to a decision. The record shows him being somewhat harassed by the Jewish religious authorities into finally sending this prisoner for execution. This Jesus was said to be dangerously popular, perhaps because the rhetoric of his teaching could move the crowds, bringing together anger at social injustice with a distinct anti-Roman edge. In Mark's account especially, there are incidents where the Jewish authorities are afraid of arresting Jesus because the populace would have rioted – the crowd had in effect protected Jesus on more than one occasion. This is why the authorities had had to resort to nighttime maneuvers and betrayal by a paid special agent to arrest him securely. But Pilate had in due course been presented with this prisoner Jesus, and having cross-examined him, he was evidently puzzled. The seasoned Roman governor could recognize a dangerous threat to the state when he saw one, but this man was a threat to nobody; in fact he seemed to be in a world of his own.

As if this wasn't enough, Pilate's wife had apparently been attracted to Jesus, and had suffered bad dreams at the thought of executing this holy man.[66] Romans were intensely superstitious, and Pilate may have been reluctant to anger a local deity by any act of gratuitous injustice. It would have created a bad omen. So it is certainly plausible that Pilate was at first momentarily persuaded to send Jesus for execution but almost immediately was left uneasy about his decision. So when an influential member of the national council, Joseph of Arimathea, came soon after, begging for the man's body, maybe Pilate thought it prudent after all to accede to his request, provided it could all be done quietly. The decision to grant burial according to Jewish rites was in itself quite a concession, quite a departure from standard procedures. Maybe in this way he could, in the end, have it both ways. Was Pilate making it just look as if Jesus had been executed? Or had he belatedly hoped to spare him after all, by allowing him to be taken down from the cross earlier than usual?

All of this is shrouded in uncertainty. There are strands of possible logic here and there; the four narratives are peppered with hints, but nothing is conclusive. The sudden decision to take him down from the cross early meant that the burial had to be a hasty affair because the Sabbath was coming on fast, so Jesus in the end was deposited in a tomb intended for someone else. It has even been argued that there were medicaments in the sponge which Jesus was given which quickly knocked him out, leading him to give up the struggle very shortly afterwards.[67] Maybe this, plus the horrific lacerations on his head and the long gash in his side, is why he seemed to be already dead when the soldiers checked soon after, making it unnecessary to break his legs – the usual brutal way to hasten a merciful death through asphyxiation. One recent medical opinion is that Jesus may have been suffering from a pleural effusion – internal bleeding of the pleura, the lining of the chest cavity – perhaps brought on by the beating he had received from the guards. Perhaps it was the build-up of blood and fluid arising from this which was released by the gash from the spear.[68] Strangely, the spear blow may then have saved his life by making him appear to be already dead. Many of the details of the four accounts fairly tease us to speculate about this detail or that, yet in the end they can only ever remain uncertain.

So was this a story about grief-induced hallucination expressing a deeper truth about the victory of the Kingdom? Or did Jesus physically survive the ordeal and come back to comfort and inspire his followers? The four narratives together give several accounts of meeting Jesus after the crucifixion, and although they seem to contradict each other in some places, some accounts do contain detail which has an authentic ring about it. Perhaps the most poignant is the encounter with Thomas when Jesus says to him, Go right ahead – have a good look at the scars; put your hand inside the gash in my side.[69] Given all this and given the possibilities about Pilate's motivation just mentioned, the case for his survival might seem quite strong. The well-attested accounts that he had been taken down from the cross early seem to lend further support to this idea.

But other accounts of the post-crucifixion encounters do feel insubstantial and even ghostly. Geza Vermes argues that the evidence, taken together, would hardly stand up in a court of law.[70] So this again is a matter of relative probability at best. Once again we are back to uncertainty, and this uncertainty does seem to be a key message which the writers evidently wanted to leave us with. Doctrines and their polished certainties came whole centuries later.

But death can be more than just physical annihilation; strange to say, it can go deeper than that. Could it be that Jesus had survived his ordeal bodily but nevertheless had undergone death in a deeper sense? When the very core of our sense of self is crushed within us, when the light of hope is extinguished and we feel utterly forsaken, something in us does indeed die. Perhaps it was his intense trust in his Abba which had finally been snuffed out as he lost consciousness. Here was his whole new vision of humanity, and the sense of his own mission and purpose which had grown in him since childhood, finally evaporating into nothing. This dark night of the soul is an experience which other mystics have spoken of. It seems that he had been stripped of everything – his self-confidence, his very sense of self – until nothing was left except a visceral clinging to something beyond him at a level below the threshold of his consciousness. Then the blessing of Abba's presence may have slowly surfaced again in him as he lay waking up in the tomb, and suddenly in a flash of exhilaration he recognized what this must mean. Others would take time to see it, but for Jesus himself this was a victory over death itself, dramatically confirming the victory of the inner Kingdom.

Maybe if we focus our attention on the literal medical facts we miss the point entirely. Modern logic reduces to the question 'Was he brain dead – yes or no?', but this kind of fact can prove nothing and can be the foundation for nothing. It's the meaning attached to an experience which gives it the power of myth to move the heart, and this meaning surely can have come only from the teaching. The events of the crucifixion had dramatized the self-giving creator whose love overwhelms our imprisoning ego, and Jesus' experience of coming back from an experience of death then expressed beautifully the victory of his Kingdom of love and trust over the menacing power of death. Perhaps our modern, literal mindset misses the drama and human depth which people saw in the story at the time.

One modern theologian has argued that this deeper symbolic meaning of resurrection only really comes home to us today when we experience it directly in our own lives.[71] Once we have gone through the fierce blows of life, like the grief of loss or the trauma of life-menacing sickness, and we come out on the other side, life afterwards can become deeper, and somehow we can appreciate and accept life more fully. This insight that resurrection can only have meaning for us as we live it is not far from Paul's way of seeing it. In turn this ties the idea of resurrection into the experience of second birth, a powerfully transforming rhythm in the experience of living, the inner Kingdom again and again bringing us back to the exhilaration of renewed life.

Perhaps this is the key connecting the Kingdom teaching and the story of the passion events. Indeed, as pagans saw in later times, dying and rising again is the very rhythm of the whole creation, echoed in the seasons of the year and even in the rhythm of every day. This is why Easter, the great pagan springtime celebration of the return of life, became the great festival of the Christian year in the west. The great mysterious dance of all things is the dance of birth, flourishing, decline and death, recycling and unifying everything, reflecting all things in all things, to the end of time. As individuals in time we die, but in God, our deeper anchoring reality, we are timeless, eternal. The story of Jesus' resurrection echoes a very ancient wisdom.

Finally, if we can see Jesus' resurrection as a symbolic truth told with mythic power, we can look again in a similar way at the doctrine of his second coming. Reinterpreting the second coming symbolically is part of the achievement of the German theologian Jürgen Moltmann. Moltmann's own journey started as he stood in the ruins of Hamburg in 1945 at a point when the whole world he had known seemed lost (like the experience of the early disciples). In the vision which he revived, the teaching of Jesus' Kingdom becomes a manifesto for all humankind which can take us beyond war and peace, beyond our current obsession with materialism, into a future which we cannot see but in which we will not be without a compass, our inner guide constantly at work within us. As we walk into this future, hope can stay alive – a hope that one day every man will live under his own fig tree, in peace and unafraid.

Chapter 12
The Logic of Parting

The ascension story is mentioned by Mark, and twice by Luke, once in his Gospel and again in his Acts of the Apostles,[72] but ignored by Matthew and John. In the common culture of the time, people were familiar with stories of semi-divine figures being taken up into the heavens as a sign of the favor of the gods, who of course lived beyond the stars. Heracles had ascended to heaven to be with the gods. Elijah was taken up in a whirlwind at the end of his prophetic life. If Jesus was God's special prophet, some would expect him to finish his work by being taken up to the heavens in a similar way.

Still, here too the biblical records are candidly uncertain. Mark is formulaic, even comically literal: 'So after talking with them the Lord Jesus was taken up into heaven and took his seat at the right hand of God.' Luke's two accounts are more cautious. The Acts of the Apostles says that 'he was lifted up before their very eyes, and a cloud took him from their sight'. The account in Luke's Gospel puts it rather beautifully like this: 'Then he led them out as far as Bethany, and blessed them with uplifted hands; and in the act of blessing he parted from them.'

Today, people who believe in God usually no longer picture him living in a place above the stars. God is seen as eternal, beyond the limits of space and time. It therefore makes little sense to see Jesus literally rising in the clear morning air like a space rocket. In a post-Copernican world, pictures of the ascension simply make no literal sense. Nowadays people might see him as somehow exiting space and time, but the manner of how this happens no longer matters. I suppose he exited space and time, if that's the right phrase, in the same way that we all do. But this still leaves us with a further persistent question. If

Jesus was indeed alive after his crucifixion, and if he did indeed meet with some of his closest followers, what happened to him after that? Not surprisingly, various legends have sprung up in response to this question.

The Jewish rebellion against Roman authority was not fought alone. Judea lay not far from the eastern edge of Roman rule, and its traditional sponsor and befriender was the historic rival and enemy of Rome, the Persian Empire. (This puts a number of things in a rather different light, does it not – from the three wise men to Pontius Pilate's deliberations? The Romans instinctively saw the Jews as allies of their old adversary Persia.) There are stories that Jesus fled eastwards to Persia[73] and in one form of the story his mother Mary went with him but died soon after arriving. Some say that a mausoleum was built in her honor (near Saveh in modern Iran). There is even a Muslim story that Jesus traveled east and died many years later in one of the valleys of Kashmir among a tribe known as the Beni Israel, who called him Yus Assaf, 'the healer'. Were the Beni Israel descendants of loyal Jewish troops sent by a Persian emperor some centuries before to stabilize his eastern frontier? Life for Jesus in Roman Palestine would no doubt be dangerous from now on, and the journey to safety in neighboring Persia would be perfectly feasible. The tomb of Yus Assaf can be visited today in Srinagar, the capital of Indian Kashmir.

But, with apologies to friends in Kashmir, stories of this do seem to miss the key point. Christian people believe that Jesus is alive today but not in the same literal sense that you and I are alive, that is, just for a limited span. The lines of an evangelical song perhaps get closer to the heart of the matter:

You ask me how I know He lives?
He lives within my heart.[74]

This classical era Jewish teacher lives on in the hearts of people today because he means so much to them, and because he transforms the way they see themselves and their lives. His Kingdom of Heaven has come alive in them.

Breaking the Prison Bars

Close to the heart of Jesus' vision was the idea that the central obstacle to human liberation was the ego, the me-me-me within us. If God was the antidote to this, then the Kingdom of Heaven was a realm of truth and love which transcended the limits of the human ego. He himself had been scorched by the fire of a transforming experience which had rendered the preoccupations of the everyday world insipid and tiresome by comparison. It is this experience which in time seems to have led him to forget his own ego and to begin to leave it behind.

Remember that all the evidence suggests Jesus had a very strong charismatic personality. Maybe little by little he began to see that the very strength of this personality was becoming a barrier, and that he needed to bring the spirit of this forgiving, self-forgetting Abba to life more directly in the way he lived each day. Like some mystics before and after him, it was in letting go of his own ego that he became one with this ego-less God. This perhaps is where he may have started to enact the role of this God as he saw him. 'The Father and I are one,' he says in John's account.[75] This is to see right through the feeling of separateness that the ego generates. If all is God then maybe God alone really and truly *is* enough.

As Mark Tully explains, any Hindu would instantly recognize what was happening here.[76] Loosing the bonds of the self is a common coinage in the Hindu path to union with the mystery of the creation, union with God, and is practiced by many sages and spiritual guides. And Jesus made it clear that all of us, if we chose to, could follow him into this union, this second birth, this inner Kingdom of the heart in which the ego no longer dominated. Some Muslim analyses of Jesus echo this, but with a distinctive insight: insofar as you escape your ego, you become closer to your real self, and this by nature is compassionate, as your creator is compassionate. Only your ego blocks this natural compassion. In Muslim words, you are attaining the Real.

Jesus seems to have seen this final fading of his ego in an oddly literal way. This is illustrated, for example, in his remarks about Judgment Day, when he sees himself rewarding those who fed him when he was hungry, clothed him when he was naked and visited him when he was in prison. Looking at each other doubtfully, these good people ask him, Exactly when did we ever do these things for you? If you did this to the least of my brothers, he replies, you did it to me.[77]

This may also throw another light on his final act of giving himself at the end of his life. Quite possibly he knew deep down inside himself that sooner or later, if he carried on challenging the religious authorities in the way he did, they would arrest him and try to have him executed by the Romans. But other considerations perhaps came into this. Aware of the human magnetism of his own personality, Jesus from quite early on had been wary of people flattering him or worshipping him in person. People kept coming up and touching him! We can understand his frustration – people were missing the point. It wasn't about his charisma; it was about a Kingdom available to everyone. At some point he may have begun to sense that ironically the very strength of his personality was distracting people, even his disciples, holding them back from bringing this Kingdom fully to life within their own lives.

In this way perhaps the great paradox slowly dawned on him. In order to bring his Kingdom to life in other people, in order to make people stand on their own feet, he had to leave them. This time of learning and proclaiming had come to its own natural conclusion. Today we may well wonder whether this short, intense period of personal and emotional turmoil, coming to a climax so early in his life, may have even burnt him out, such was its fierce intensity.

So it was with careful deliberation that he prepared his followers for life after he had gone, reassuring them that the inner presence of Abba would remain with them, too, that in the form of the Holy Spirit he would come alive within them. After that, there was nothing else for Jesus to do but to go. He had completed his work. In the accounts of his entry into Jerusalem on the back of an ass and then his provocation at the temple, there are the signs of carefully planned ceremony, deliberately provoking the powers that be. The last Passover meal together, the last supper, has all the dramatic resonances of a conscious leave-taking. How intensely human, brimming with emotion as he faced his own imminent death, to say to his beloved followers, Where two or three of you are gathered in my name, there I am among you.

Somewhere along the way, the two ideas had finally come together. He would go, and he would do that by delivering himself up to the authorities, who would have got him sooner or later in any case, and in doing this he would demonstrate his ego-transcending Kingdom in action, fulfilling in one dramatic event the truth he had felt called to carry out. How right he was that words on their own were not enough to express the power of this extraordinary vision! It would reach out to people everywhere only when it was followed through in an unforgettable act of self-giving. It might take people a while to see it, but he would have demonstrated much more than just the sordid limits of Roman political power. In his action would be embodied the soaring truth of a self-giving creator in solidarity with suffering humanity in all ages, the supremely paradoxical victory of powerless indestructible love. Clearly, everyday logic has been left far behind. This is sublime logic. It's about reaching out and finally tackling the exile in the human heart.

To many of us today, this is a strange logic from another place, persuasive perhaps for some, for others just altogether too strange. Yet for all its strangeness, it can still touch us at deep levels beneath the conscious mind, levels where creativity is nurtured and dreams are hatched but where our domineering, limited ego cannot reach.

So where do we meet Jesus today, this Jesus who bursts the bounds of the imprisoning human ego with the liberating news of his inner Kingdom? This is not about admiring him or even worshipping him; it is about following him, as he challenged us to do. It's about seeing through the bounds of our own ego and the delusion of being alone which it keeps in place. To paraphrase Albert Schweitzer's celebrated conclusion, [78] we meet him in the experiences which bind us together in the rush and stress of the workaday world, in the pains and triumphs of relationships and of raising children. We see him in the faces of those we rub shoulders with in the process of getting through each day, and in the eyes of those whose lives we touch in a thousand un-noticed ways every single day we live.

This classical era Jewish visionary saw right through the human heart and came out into a landscape which no one else had even imagined, a landscape up and away beyond the constricting walls of the ego. From this new landscape, he holds out to us a new understanding of who we are and a new way of facing an uncertain future, with a refreshing breeze of hope.

There is life beyond the ego. The inner Kingdom first seen by Jesus reaches through the prison bars of the self, uniting us with each other in something closer that just a community, something which Paul called 'one body' in Christ Jesus. Strange and compelling in the same breath. You ask me how I know he lives? He lives within my heart. And the heart is bigger and freer and carries more promise than the ego ever could.

Part Four
Christianity

Part Four provides a historical bridge pointing forward to the dilemmas of the modern faith. Chapter 13 ponders the underlying logic of the Christmas story, and then gives examples of the unique fusion of cultures which characterized early Christianity. It takes a view of how Christianity arose as a Greek understanding of a Jewish inspiration, synthesizing early memories of Jesus' teaching and interpretations of the events of the passion.

Part Four then goes on to outline a few of the more pivotal events in Christian history up to the present day. Chapter 14 documents an ironic shift in attitudes to Roman power in early centuries, from initial hostility and challenge to later accommodation and alliance. It then traces the sometimes dire consequences of the onset of the Dark Ages on the western church. Chapter 15 finally attempts to catch something of the sweep of events in recent centuries and the daunting challenges presented by the modern world.

Chapter 13
What Others Made of Him

A Birth of Hope

'A young woman is with child, and she will give birth to a son and call him Immanuel.' These words from the prophet Isaiah, quoted again in Matthew's account of Jesus' birth, actually catch the central meaning of Jesus' entire teaching in one single word, one single name: Immanuel, 'God with us'. [79] For this was a teaching which brought the passionate, overwhelming presence of the creator of all things right in among us. This was no distant emperor on his sky-throne; this was a power alive within all creation including the human heart, caring for the sparrow and the grass of the fields and for every one of us too.

The experience of this presence within the heart, this second birth, had evidently transformed Jesus himself, and this experience is recognized in the Gospel narratives as the start of his teaching mission. In Matthew's account Jesus sees the spirit of God descending like a dove to alight on him as he comes up out of the river Jordan.[80] Luke dates this important event with ceremony and precision, telling us that it took place in the fifteenth year of the reign of the emperor Tiberius.[81] In one sense this second birth is the one that mattered.

Of course the magic of the biblical birth narratives arises because, looking back, we all know what the birth of Jesus as a baby was to lead to. It's this hindsight which gives the story its drama, and the series of acclamations which Luke puts into the mouths of Miriam/Mary, Zechariah and Simeon all speak of a birth of hope for new beginnings. To celebrate Christmas, then, means to celebrate this birth of hope which we all know Jesus was later to proclaim.

Today the whole point of this story is often less clear. People still picture the birth of a demigod, half human and half god; in fact many people still seem to think that they have to believe that Jesus' biological father was God the Holy Spirit! We can easily forget that Christian doctrine insists on Jesus' full humanity. Matthew's account of the birth clearly traces Jesus' ancestry through his father Joseph, and Luke appears to agree, referring almost dismissively to 'a girl betrothed to a man named Joseph, a descendant of David; the girl's name was Mary'.[82] It's true that Matthew tells us that Mary had realized she was pregnant before the marriage, causing Joseph to hesitate about going ahead with the legal ceremonies. Luke's account on the other hand, can be read in a more straightforward fashion: Mary has a vision, and is told that the power of the most high will overshadow her, but there is no unambiguous indication that the pregnancy will be unusually early.[83] Still, the mystery and wonder of unexplainable things adds to the mood of expectation as the story unfolds.

Jewish and Greek traditions were in fact both used to situations in which unexpected or miraculous births are attributed to the intervention of a god, but there was an important difference between the two traditions. In the Greek and Roman world the god usually fathers the child in a more or less literal fashion – Plato, Alexander the Great, Julius Caesar and others were said to have been fathered in this way. Miraculous births in the Jewish tradition, by contrast, have a different feel about them. This God is no superhuman creature, but a creator who works *through* his creatures. On the whole the Jewish tradition therefore expects a human father to have made his contribution! Nevertheless, this God of Israel could close the womb and open it again, sometimes against all expectations, and there are several examples of this in the stories of the patriarchs and elsewhere in the Hebrew scriptures.

This sense of mystery and expectation is strengthened by four strange additions to Matthew's genealogy of Jesus' ancestry. The author goes out of his way to include in his list of male ancestors the names of four women, three of whom, Tamar, Rahab and Ruth, were foreign, and one of whom, Bathsheba, was certainly married to a foreigner and was possibly foreign herself too. Three of these women gave birth in controversial or even scandalous circumstances to heirs who would go on to play a significant role in Israel's history. There may be a hint in this that the birth of Jesus was good news for foreigners and not just for the people of Israel. But is there also just a whiff of alarm here? Is the God of Israel courting scandal once again, as he had done in the past?

The idea of virgin birth was in fact quite familiar in the neighboring cultures of the time. In Nabatea, for example, south-east of Palestine, a god named Dusares was called the 'only begotten' of the Lord, his mother was said to be a virgin, and his feast day was 25 December!

But in any case, Jewish tradition at the time understood virginity quite differently, sometimes apparently a case of legal status, simply describing a girl's non-married status, at other times referring to her actual age.[84] Isaiah's original foretelling, quoted at the start of this chapter, is of a young woman conceiving and giving birth to a child. This was then expressed in the Greek translation of the Jewish scriptures, the Septuagint, by a word which likewise means 'young woman' but can sometimes mean 'virgin', in what must surely be one of the most fateful translations in human history. This is a good example of a story from one culture being understood differently in another, a characteristic of early Christianity.

Today the celebration of the birth of Jesus is still widely expressed in literal terms, thanks partly to the effect that hymns and carols can have of fossilizing the story in words which may no longer carry natural conviction for us today: 'Veiled in flesh the Godhead see[85] ...'

It's tempting to observe that things are confusing enough already and that using archaic language like this simply adds to the confusion. Nevertheless, despite the quaint language, the joyous explosion of the Christian response to Christmas can still be authentic, a fit response of the heart to the freeing of the human spirit which Jesus proclaimed.

As it happens, the date of 25 December was eventually borrowed in the fourth century from the feast of the redeemer Sol Invictus, the 'Unconquered Sun', in a gesture which speaks volumes, acknowledging the advent of the light of Jesus the Sun in the midst of our winter darkness. (Does this fusion of traditions survive today in the figure of the Celtic cross: the signs of the sun and the cross brought together in one symbol?) Christmas, then, is something to be enjoyed as a truly Christian *and* pagan commemoration, the ancient winter solstice celebrations within and alongside the Christian festival.

Why did Matthew and Luke consider the story of Jesus' birth worth including in their narratives? Mark, after all, had paid it no attention, and later John was to ignore it likewise. Jesus' whole teaching was to be about new beginnings, a second birth of hope in the human heart. Had these two authors felt the power of this second birth in themselves, and did they tell the story of the birth of the baby in order to reflect the magic of new creation?

Today the magic of any birth can still be overwhelming when we consider the awesome detail of what we now know about the processes involved. When we ponder the explosive, high-speed, minutely coordinated development of the embryo from the very moment of conception to the emergence of this tiny, brand new, defenseless wonder, suddenly the grandeur and wonder of it all can strike us. In celebrating the birth of the baby in the story, we also glimpse the glory of how we ourselves are created and the awesome mystery of who we are.

At Christmas, then, we celebrate both the wonder of our first birth, and the promise – the work in progress – of our second birth. In one festival we celebrate our creation and our completion, our origin and our destination.

Jewish Roots

It is a striking feature of Jesus, and a witness to his absorption in the heat of his own vision, that although his teaching had such clear appeal and implications for humanity in all cultures, Jesus himself appears not to have seen this at first, or not to have seen its full significance. To say this seems at first sight surprising, some might even say scandalous, but we need to be wary of seeing him as omniscient and therefore incapable of learning. To think like this is surely to call into question his full humanity if this is to have any meaning at all in our own time. But the evidence speaks for itself. Again and again his major concern is to renew Israel, which would then be a light to the nations, rather than to evangelize the pagan world directly.

Jesus had evidently come up through a broad movement of Jewish aspiration for liberation as a people, then increasingly became aware of the limitations of this, and finally set out on a momentous journey in which he reached out for a very much wider vision. In fact Jesus' very use of a political metaphor, the Kingdom, to express what became an essentially internal idea, is a candid witness to the partly political origins of his thinking. This is further confirmed by the evident political understanding which some of his followers took from his teaching. Even in the departure scene depicted in the Acts of the Apostles, the very last question his followers put to Jesus is about a very political Kingdom: 'Lord, is this the time at which you are to restore sovereignty to Israel?'[86]

It took other remarkable minds to see that this was truly a message for all humanity. Paul has, after all, been called the founder of Christianity, not without a degree of justice, given the crucial influence of his thinking on the early movement and how it understood Jesus. Paul's thinking circles round the problem, the daunting problem, of translating this profoundly Jewish vision with its central political metaphor into the terms of thought of a Greek-speaking, pagan world ruled by Romans who were edgily suspicious of anyone using the language of liberation movements. But it was left to John a few decades later to make an even bigger leap of the imagination. The very light with which we are born was first recognized and proclaimed by this man from Nazareth in Galilee province. It is because this teaching reflects this light and speaks directly to the heart that Jesus can speak to people in all cultures and in all ages.

One natural fault line which emerged in the very earliest years of the new faith was that between those who had known Jesus, all of them presumably Jewish Christians, and those involved in the wider world beyond Palestine, very few of whom had ever met Jesus and who probably knew really very little about him. Paul, who is making converts across the Greek-speaking world up to 20 years before the first Gospels appear, doesn't seem primarily interested in the detail of Jesus' teachings. He seems more preoccupied with the saving effect of his self-giving on all humankind.

Perhaps the universalizing theology of Paul, John, and others like the author of the letter to the Hebrews may have inadvertently fed an early trend away from the real person of Jesus, a trend later taken up by Gnostics. The narratives of Mark and then Matthew and Luke reassert the treasured memory of Jesus and his teaching in vivid detail, and perhaps this represents a counter-move to this trend and an attempt to find a center ground in the threatening split.

More importantly, these three narratives started to be written down and edited at around the time of, or shortly after, the Roman attack on Jerusalem in 70 CE in which the temple had been razed to the ground, a seismic event for the young movement. The Jerusalem church, led by James the brother of Jesus, was still a natural anchor for all Christians everywhere and presumably had strong Jewish Christian associations. It seems likely that it would have been dispersed in the wake of this Roman action, and this event may have threatened the very survival of the oral records of the memory of Jesus; hence the sudden urgency to set it all down in writing. A decade or two further on, John's narrative seems to take a more balanced, distanced point of view, taking inspiration from both sides, including authentic detail from Jesus' life and teaching yet also seeing its significance within a much wider setting.

In later centuries, ironically, the trend towards seeing Jesus as an immensely powerful cosmic figure was to emerge triumphant, yet in their own time all four narrative Gospels in their different ways succeeded in establishing Jesus as a very distinctive human being.

There is documentary evidence from the second century of the continuing existence of strict Jewish followers of Jesus, variously referred to as Nazarenes or Ebionites,[87] who kept the Law and saw Jesus as the great renewer and simplifier of the Law, the second Moses. (The long speech given by Stephen before his killing, reported in Luke's Acts of the Apostles, gives a flavor of this early first-century point of view.[88]) In Palestine itself, Jewish followers of Jesus, as Jews, would soon enough be hounded by the Roman authorities after the succession of Jewish national revolts culminating in the final razing of the whole city of Jerusalem in 135 CE.

Some settled southwards, towards Nabatea, at a safer distance from Roman power. As late as the early fourth century they are mentioned by orthodox Christian writers. Then they seem to fade from history until just a few centuries later, when Muhammad encountered Jewish clans in Medina and elsewhere in north-west Arabia. There appears to have been a variety of free Christian and/or Jewish communities, safe from the long arm of Roman orthodoxy in the north. Were some of these Nazareans? Could it be that their reverence for their great prophet, their second Moses, survives today within the Jesus suras of Muhammad's great recitation, the Qur'an?[89] More recently, one author mentions an Arabic document discovered late in the twentieth century in Khuzistan, in south-west Iran, indicating the existence of a Nazarean community as late as the tenth century CE. [90]

A New Faith for Pagans

Only a generation after Jesus' execution, other followers of Jesus, first called 'Christians' in the large cosmopolitan city of Antioch in northern Syria, found themselves influenced by dramatically changing circumstances. After the Romans had sacked Jerusalem and destroyed the temple, Jewish metaphors taken from political liberation movements had become dangerous, and increasingly hard for ex-pagans to understand anyway. Talk of a Kingdom would then perhaps begin to lose ground, while a faith told more in terms of Greek culture began to take shape.

One interesting example of the interpenetration of Jewish and Greek cultures is in the narratives of Mark's and Luke's Gospels, where they use story elements and characterizations from the epic poems of Homer, as mentioned earlier in Chapter 2.[91] Like Poseidon, Jesus calms the seas, and like Nestor he feeds multitudes on a shoreline. Even in the account of his death there are striking parallels: some bystanders mock him, some women mourn him from afar, friends rescue his body and bury him properly, and he returns from Hades alive. Likewise in Luke's Acts of the Apostles there are accounts of sea voyages, dreams, prison escapes and other incidents reminiscent of the two great seminal poems.

Redemption cults were growing in the Roman world of the time, as the appeal of often local polytheistic beliefs slowly began to weaken. The worship of Mithras the redeemer sun god, originally from Zoroastrian Persia, swept through the length of the empire and was especially favored in the Roman army.[92] (A large Mithras temple was uncovered in the city of London some years ago, and others can be visited elsewhere in England, for example close to Hadrian's Wall in Northumberland.) Redemption became a major theme also in the new Christianity, as worship and publicly attested belief in Jesus the redeemer became its central requirement. Mithraism also had a hierarchy of priests and a ritual involving bread, wine and water.

Greek culture, too, was familiar with stories of gods and goddesses descending to earth to conceive children with human partners, and the resulting children were special, favored with divine power.[93] Matthew and Luke give us birth stories for Jesus which are in some ways similar, providing convincing evidence at the time attesting both to his humanity and to his god-like origins. Heroic figures in Greek mythology also visited the world of the dead, and in Christian creeds Jesus does something very similar. Perhaps above all, the idea of a god dying and then rising back to life in order to renew the life of the people was already a cult in the neighboring Roman province of Egypt and elsewhere. This became the very heart of the new faith. It has even been argued that the later cult of Mary the Virgin was driven forward with especial fervor in Ephesus, one of the two or three very largest cities of the early Roman world. Ephesus was a center of the cult of the virgin goddess Diana, and some writers point to striking similarities between the cult of Diana and the cult of Mary the Virgin.

What became Christianity was thus a Greek take on an original Jewish vision, a fusion between the two quite different cultural traditions which was very characteristic of its time. This is in no sense to condemn this development. Given the potential universal appeal of Jesus' vision and the cultural difference between Jewish and Greek worlds, the development has an air of inevitability about it.

Some insights of the new faith confirmed the original teaching while others added startling new force to it. This is from one of the letters to Timothy:

The love of money is the root of all evil, and in pursuit of it
some have ... spiked themselves on many a painful thorn.
But you ... must shun all that ... Run the great race of faith
and take hold of eternal life, for to this you were called ...[94]

An appealing image for a young Greek male, don't you think,
running the great race of faith, like an Olympic athlete? At the
same time, quite clearly the pursuit of money and eternal life are
still seen as radically incompatible, clearly echoing the original
teaching. Much more powerful, this is Paul writing in words
which reverberate perhaps especially today: 'There is no such
thing as Jew and Greek, slave and freeman, male and female; for
you are all one person in Christ Jesus.'[95] This is truly revolutionary language, laying the foundations of an entirely new
world, in some ways brilliantly enhancing the original vision but
decidedly changing its center of gravity.

For the first century or so, the new movement seems to have
made slow progress, but then in its second century it appears to
have taken off to some degree, spreading more rapidly across the
Greek world and bringing in increasing numbers of non-Jews. It
is perhaps worth pausing here for a moment to appreciate the
scale of this second-century achievement. To make converts in
less civilized areas, like the western provinces – Gaul or
Britannia, for example – would have been less remarkable. To
have caught the imagination of the major centers of the Greek-
speaking world was an achievement of an altogether higher
order. This was intellectually one of the most advanced cultures
on the surface of the earth, and although some argue that it was
past its high point by this time, its sophistication was still very
much alive.

But in the end the dazzling culture of Homer, Plato,
Aristophanes, the Stoics – all the tradition of natural philosophy
and so much more – was won over to a teaching which may have
seemed to Greek eyes at first sight somewhat unsophisticated but

which offered something which their own culture, for all its achievements, couldn't reach. The Greek philosophical schools had attracted thousands among the ruling and educated classes in the east and also in Rome itself, but their appeal was characteristically intellectual and in the end affected only limited numbers. This new faith was for everyone. It seems to have had a mass emotional appeal. It was implicitly more egalitarian, it was still instinctively skeptical or even hostile to Roman power, and it was interested in compassion as well as justice. Perhaps above all, it answered aspirations and fears lying deeper in the heart.

But as the new faith grew, it changed, migrating from its original Jewish context into a still pagan Greek culture with different ways of thinking and very different problems to solve. Perhaps it expanded too fast for its own good. From its small-scale beginnings it became a major religion of a whole civilization across the length of the Roman Empire and to an extent also in Persia, stretching over huge land masses. Fragmentation and division were almost bound to be by-products of this rapid growth and dispersal.

At some point, sadly, it shed much of its founder's non-violence. A dark shadow fell across this faith. In the course of the centuries, its response to perceived enemies became noted for its periodic extreme violence and intolerance, like a black sabbath reversal of the spirit of the Kingdom of the heart.

Chapter 14
Ironies of Time

Over these last two millennia, Christianity has seen a mixture of continuity and cumulatively radical change. It has been scarred by the sometimes savage events of history and, on occasion, distorted by failures of its own making. This chapter contains a series of brief glimpses and is in no sense a balanced account; on the contrary it focuses on the negative side of things quite deliberately. It does so in the hope that we might better understand the road this faith has traveled and something of the state it has reached by now. Perhaps the dark pessimistic view of human nature which Christianity sometimes still tends to convey is in part an echo of some of the grim history it has come through since its founding.

The Roman Imperium

It was very early indeed in its history that the first signs of discord became evident between an infant Christian community and an already transforming Jewish faith, both expanding across the eastern Roman Empire and the borders of Persia further to the east. For quite some time this does seem to have been a dispute between brothers, much of it centering on different interpretations of the Jewish scriptures. Perhaps this was bound to be contentious – startlingly, the new community appeared to be distancing itself from the faith which had nourished its founder.

Soon enough, Christian communities would have to undergo ferocious persecution mainly because of their principled refusal to worship the emperor. Within just a few decades, though, the people of Israel would have to live through much worse. First came the destruction of the temple by the Roman general Titus in 70 CE – but this was no more than a precursor. Two generations later came the ultimate catastrophe, truly the original holocaust, with the genocidal slaughter and dispersal of Jews from Jerusalem and much of their ancestral homeland under the emperor Hadrian in the wake of the Bar Kokhba revolt of the early 130s. (According to some estimates, up to half a million people were killed as the political reality of Judea was simply eliminated, henceforth to be named Syria Palestina. Even holy Jerusalem was razed and transformed into the pagan Roman city of Aelia Capitolina.)

Amid such terrible events Christians seem to have forgotten much of the spirit of Jesus' teaching exemplified in his story of the good Samaritan. This forgetfulness was to set a bleak historical precedent. Much later in Europe, the churches repeatedly failed to respect the older covenant, casting a long and dark shadow over a Christian civilization. This failure is all the more shameful when compared with a more careful respect for both Christian and Jewish minorities under Muslim rule in later times.

If the issue of separation from Judaism was a major preoccupation during the first century, the real battle for the soul of the new faith would be a feature of the next two centuries. This was already getting underway as the Gospels were being written in the late first century, and only came to a final resolution a few decades before the emperor's council at Nicea in 322 CE. Although there was a whole series of other doctrinal disputes during this time, the great enduring struggle was that between what was to become orthodox Christianity and the whole range of Gnostic world-views. Gnosticism was fundamentally preoccupied with the individual's path to personal knowledge of the divine. It represented a broad consensus in its time across a whole cosmopolitan culture, reflecting ideas not only from Greek philosophy but also from Egypt, Zoroastrian Persia and possibly also Buddhist India, and all of this was brought to bear on the emerging new faith.

The Gnostic world-view had attractive and less attractive sides to it. It was often deep and subtle in its understanding of the spiritual life and apparently was constitutionally anarchic, contrasting with the increasingly organized structures of authority in the orthodox church itself. At the same time Gnostics tended to elitism and secret interpretations of scriptural sayings, and to despise the body and all things physical. In the end the orthodox faith had a vital social dimension and was more clearly a faith for everyone, not just for the religiously inclined. Still, the quest for spiritual depth so central to the early Gnostics was to be carried forward in different forms in later centuries, for example in the monastic movements and in the periodic re-emergence of Christian mysticism. Some of its spirit is recognizable also in later Islamic culture, especially perhaps in the flowering of Sufism, with its yearning for a mystical personal union with God.

When victory finally came for the hierarchies of the orthodox church, however, there followed a serious attempt to expunge this by now hated heresy from the historical record. The remarkable haul of writings found near Nag Hammadi in Upper Egypt in the 1940s, greatly enriching our understanding of the early Christian world, had evidently been hastily buried to avoid one of the many book burnings of the time. The light of a tolerant, diverse Greek culture was beginning to fail, and perhaps an early ominous symptom of this was the sight of Christians burning Christian books.

Not long after, and by now almost three centuries after Jesus, came a further serious failure of vision, comparable in the scale of its consequences to the earlier break with the Jewish faith. The new emperor, Constantine, a western pagan brought up in far-off Britannia, after something like a conversion experience in 312 CE had evidently decided that it made strategic sense to make Christianity an officially favored religion, in effect bringing its leaders close to the political power structure of his empire.

Among other things, he no doubt liked its organized, hierarchical structure of authority, and shrewdly he realized that he could turn this growing force from a worrying rival into an ally of state power. It is possible that Constantine was also wary of this faith's earlier reputation as a focus for anti-empire sentiment, and as a superstitious man he may have been keen to acquire the favor of its evidently powerful God.

Perhaps this kind of development was inevitable sooner or later. Given the continuous popular expansion of the Christian faith among the people, it was perhaps only a matter of time before one emperor or another would decide to adopt it rather than fight it. Perhaps the logic of hard imperial realpolitik and the Kingdom not of this world were bound to encounter each other sooner or later.

After centuries of periodically vicious persecution – the latest and the most savage outbreaks under Diocletian still recent and vivid within the memory of older people still alive at the time – this move by Constantine must certainly have seemed like the most spectacular answer to prayer. There is evidence that some Christians still thought of the Kingdom of Heaven partly in political terms and welcomed the new friendship of the emperor as its final success and vindication!

Nevertheless it must have occurred to others at the time that this surely represented a denial of Jesus' crucial early teaching from the desert: his principled refusal of the temptations of political power in all its manifestations. Surely this was a lethal danger, and fateful consequences would ensue. It would not be long before some church leaders began to ape the manners and the lifestyle of the imperial court and to affect an increasingly aggressive intolerance towards any attempt at dissent from fellow Christians. Heresy now threatened the unity of the empire and therefore offended the emperor personally.

For the moment, a new phenomenon arose in world history: the great Christian Empire, an immensely influential model for later rulers throughout Europe, still recognizably Christian but at the same time a grotesque fusion of the image of the gentle prophet of the inner Kingdom with the pomp and vanity and earthly glory of political power.

Rising above the high altar of San Vitale in Ravenna is a large, still brightly colored mosaic depicting the figure of Jesus dressed in sumptuous robes – purple, indicating his aristocratic rank – robes which he himself would surely have despised. Nearby on the chancel walls on either side stand the figures, richly crowned and bejeweled, of the emperor Justinian and his notorious courtesan wife Theodora, the Evita of her time, both of them decorously bowing in obeisance in the direction of Jesus. This image is so full of rich irony. Jesus would have related easily to Theodora the woman of the street before she had met the emperor, but would he have found Theodora the jaded scheming courtesan quite so easy to reach, this Lady Macbeth figure with so much innocent blood on her hands? Facing this ultimate rags-to-riches survivor, would he have advised her to sell all that she had and give it to the poor?!

This bizarre marriage of opposites did in some ways civilize the state in dangerous times, and a dialogue of sorts arose between faith and power as future rulers were schooled in Christian belief, but it also deeply compromised the faith, turning it into something it had never foreseen. This faith which had started as the ultimate challenge to earthly political power had now tied the knot with this same power in a lasting relationship of mutual obeisance and ideological support. Increasingly, the church leaders of the fourth and succeeding centuries would begin to hide behind a quasi-political authority, a deeply corrupting habit of thought which would continue to damage the faith in future ages. The Kingdom not of this world became submerged as church leaders became preoccupied with high questions of authority and social cohesion.

The Legacy of the Dark Ages

There was worse to come, as little more than half a century after the death of Constantine the power of the empire itself began to shake. Inconceivably, after over four hundred years of the encompassing security of Roman civilization came the catastrophe of comprehensive social breakdown right across the western half of this vast empire, amid wave after wave of barbarian invasions.

The first to arrive were the Goths, moving in the 370s from their heartland north of the Danube under the shock of sudden pressure from the Huns arriving from the Asian steppe to the east. The Goths tumbled into the empire in two waves, ending up several decades later as the new ruling class in both Italy and Spain, and plenty of others were to follow their highly successful example in succeeding years. Augustine's world, steeped in the considered dialogue of eastern classical thought, would not now be repeated for many centuries in the west as the civilization which supported this whole way of life came crashing down. This ushered in for most of Europe fully 600 years of violent, barbaric conditions, now accurately referred to as the Dark Ages.

Historians in recent years have nuanced our understanding of the Dark Ages, questioning the alleged excellence of late Roman civilization in the west and laying more stress on degrees of continuity between it and later times. The light of learning did flicker on in Ireland and elsewhere, and for a time Celtic influence was felt as far south as the Alps. But at some point a Gothic horde had leveled the major Roman city of Aquilegia in north-east Italy, and others throughout the west were soon to be visited by a similar fate. Then in the mid-fifth century Vandal raiders from the sea trashed even Rome itself and left it in ruins. It's true that in the sixth century the Christian Empire centered in Constantinople did manage to reconquer Italy and much of the province of Africa and even a foothold in southern Spain, but the old prosperity did not return. The Germanic invasions, although intermittent, would last fully three hundred years in themselves, ending with the Lombards, who reconquered much of Italy from the empire in the mid-seventh century. It was perhaps the cumulative effect over such a long period of time which did the real damage.

Soon Christianity in the west began to reflect the profound pessimism and insecurity of its time. Augustine, for example, seems to have shared a growing misogyny with other writers of the time, like Ambrose, his early mentor, or Jerome, the translator of the Latin Bible. His catastrophic theory that it was sexual lust which had spread the guilt of original sin like a virus down the generations is a good example of this spreading pessimism, itself infecting Christian culture right up to modern times. (The idea of inherited sin was no doubt influenced by Paul, himself reflecting an older Jewish inheritance, but the stress on the sexual side of things seems to have been pure Augustine!)

The newly emerging idea of Europe, essentially the result of repeated alliances between Frankish kings and the bishops of Rome, became a political reality, and although in its way it tried to take the old empire as its model, this new world was essentially barbarian in its roots. The great Christian Empire in the east with its awesome new cathedral of the Holy Wisdom in Constantinople easily outshone the west. Then, starting in the early eighth century, the dazzling new Muslim civilization in the east and in Spain rose to even greater heights, in sharp contrast to a western Christendom in which even the great Frankish emperor Charlemagne was, some say, practicing the art of writing his own name.

Significantly it was the civilization of Muslim Spain, al-Andalus, which did so much to breathe life into a still relatively primitive Christian Europe and to create early foundations for the later Renaissance and the eventual revival of the sciences, especially after the capture by Christian forces of the Spanish Muslim city of Toledo in 1085. It was from its great libraries, more than anywhere else, that European scholars learned about the lost works of Aristotle, about Arabic technology, for example in navigation, and about Indian numerals which were soon to make more advanced mathematics a practical reality. (Indian numerals were also introduced into Europe at about the same time by the merchant and mathematician Leonardo of Pisa, also known as Fibonacci.)

Many centuries before, Augustine himself had warned of the need to respect the findings of the natural sciences, and to avoid rushing into decisions which would later trap the faith in anti-scientific standpoints.[96] Yet when we understand the pessimism, acute insecurity and habitual violence of the intervening centuries, perhaps it makes it easier for us to understand the abject failure of the churches, starting in late Renaissance times, to maintain an open response to an entirely new kind of challenge, as the new sciences set about creating the framework of the modern world.

Today even a major sea-change like the Reformation, with all its transforming consequences for the whole continent and the endless decades of religious wars which followed in its wake, can at times seem almost like a sub-plot in this wider agenda, the challenge of an entirely new reality.

The celebrated case of Galileo may have centered on sophisticated discussion about the meaning of scientific hypotheses, but sophisticated or not, even a distinguished thinker like Galileo was forced to sign a recantation under the implied threat of physical torture, and spent his remaining years under house arrest. He would not easily forget the savage punishment meted out to his colleague and acquaintance Giordano Bruno, who had stubbornly refused to recant and had been burned in public, naked and upside down. By whose orders had this satanic, vengeful event been devised and carried out? After many centuries the leaders of the church had become far too familiar with the trappings and the attitudes of political power. The historic accommodation of the churches with the kingdoms of this world had cast a long shadow, right through the Dark Ages and into modern times.

Yet in the calamitous human weaknesses of the churches can we not recognize the same weaknesses which Jesus had put his finger on when he warned his followers against the personal ambitions so characteristic of the kingdoms of this world? Hierarchies and clear lines of authority might on occasion make good politics, but these ways had no affinity with the ways of the Kingdom of Heaven.

What we recognize as Christianity today has evidently grown from a whole succession of major influences: the pre-crucifixion teachings of Jesus, responses to the passion story, early struggles with Judaism and with Gnostic thinking, the great settlement with Constantine, the comprehensive genius of Augustine of Hippo, the long legacy of the Dark Ages, the more recent stand-off with the sciences and with the modern world more generally, and many more. Over time, it replaced the heat and the innovative charge of the original vision with the defense of an increasingly elaborate and backward-looking tradition. In this way we received a picture of Jesus largely reflecting the values of this long tradition and its instinctively authoritarian attitudes. This is the travesty discussed in the early chapters of this book.

Perhaps this rapid historical overflight has been unduly one-sided. Nevertheless the Gospel transmitted by the churches has been a somewhat altered version of the original, bringing hope and love into people's lives but at the same time oppressing them too often with a wholly disproportionate sense of guilt and helplessness, sexual neurosis and self-contempt. And as we all know, this fearful, damaged faith in its time produced the unspeakable barbarities of crusades and witch-hunts, the torture rooms of the Holy Inquisition and the shameful history of Christian Europe's treatment of its Jewish population.

Summing up, it might be fair to say that the God of the political arm, the distant God who commands, had in the intervening centuries crowded out the intimate, transforming God of Jesus, that intense experience in the heart which lay at the center of Jesus' vision. Can we really say that the immense God of later centuries, the King above the kings, the ultimate picture of power and might, found its inspiration in the teaching of Jesus? Are we serious?! Isn't this picture more like a mocking satire on his teaching, more like the nightmare he foresaw and so decisively rejected in his early desert experience?

But the same teaching of Jesus assures us that the truth and power of the inner Kingdom can survive anything that human beings do to distort it or discredit it. Kill it and it will rise again, time after time, for its promise of renewal is rooted deep in the heart.

Chapter 15
The Assault of Modernity

The Loss of the Intellectual High Ground

Given such a calamitous previous history, the later alienation of a majority population from the influence of the churches in much of Europe must surely come as no surprise. This loss of influence has ebbed and flowed throughout the twentieth century but it is really the end result of a rather longer historical process. From perhaps the late seventeenth century, as the sciences began to open up so many new realities, there began a long process whereby the churches eventually found themselves more and more at odds with this new world. I hope that the following account catches at least the main essentials of this complex sweep of events.

At first the new sciences seemed to confirm the glory of the creation in a profusion of exciting new insights. Many of the deists and rationalists of the eighteenth century would therefore have been surprised at the idea of a fundamental conflict between Christian belief and the new sciences. Reflective Christians would have agreed with Galileo that truth was to be found in the Book of Nature as well as the Book of Scripture (sometimes referred to as the book of the works of God and the book of the word of God). But as time passed, Christianity began nevertheless to find it increasingly difficult to hold together its own comprehensive explanation of reality, failing to enter into a sustained dialogue with this new, expanding source of understanding.

For a time the gravitational physics of the stars revealed by Isaac Newton was allowed as a system of secondary causation set in motion by the great First Cause, while the world of matter and of life remained largely a sacred mystery, safe from the inroads of the scientists. William Paley's argument from design – that the intricate wonder of life witnessed to the hand of a divine designer – seemed to sum it all up conclusively.

A few decades later and in a fast-changing situation, Charles Darwin's great book which launched the idea of natural selection on the world (the idea of evolution over time was a good half-century older) was met here and there with some sympathetic interest as well as hostility within the churches. James Orr, an early American fundamentalist no less, put it tellingly: 'Evolution is coming to be recognized as but a new name for creation, only that the creative power now works from within, instead of, as in the old conception, in an external, plastic fashion.'[97] Nevertheless, Darwin's central contention had to undergo sustained criticism as well as acclaim from within the sciences for some decades. Some geologists favored it; some physicists had serious theoretical objections. Before it came to be fully accepted by a large majority in the scientific community, the significance of the work of Gregor Mendel on inheritance and of Thomas Hunt Morgan and others on the gene had first to be fully appreciated. This was not finally achieved until well into the twentieth century.

The progress of the physical sciences was of course just one part of a very much wider transformation of the western thought-world, in which a continuing rise of education, a revival of interest in the culture of the ancient world, and a confidence in the enlightening power of reason transformed political aspirations, the arts and much besides. This no doubt seemed to many at the time to be like an awakening of humankind from a long slumber. Some currents within the main stream were more skeptical than others about the march of reason – the Romantic movement, for example – and church people found natural allies here and there. But it was the emerging stand-off with the sciences which seems to have been most central in challenging the churches, before long giving to them a sense of being embattled against what seemed a hostile and increasingly self-confident secular world.

This increasing difficulty over time between church and science had one major and remarkable result. Originally the great enemy had been evil; in the early centuries heresy was added to this, but as the centuries passed it seemed as if a third enemy had arisen. As the churches became increasingly embattled against major conclusions of the sciences, to many people it appeared to become more estranged from rationality itself. Of course this was not a simple process. There continued to be significant numbers of scientists who were also religious people and a number of theologians who remained devoted to a rational, open dialogue. A personality typical of the time was the village parson who was also an enthusiastic stargazer or fossil collector. But larger numbers of religious people were beginning to see the appeal of their faith not just as going beyond the limits of rationality but increasingly as superior to a merely human rationality, even at times opposed to it. Scientific reasoning itself became in some way suspect for many religious people, but at the same time it began to influence their thinking in all kinds of unexpected ways.

This sometimes had curious consequences, for example a profound change in the understanding of miracles. Instead of being seen as reminders of the continuing and ubiquitous work of the creator, part of an inherently miraculous world order, they began to be seen as events which broke the known laws of the universe. This apparent breach of rationality itself began to be seen as the hallmark of God's activity and presence, but this had the effect of making miracles really quite rare and exceptional events, and increasingly private rather than social, almost as if the creator was in retreat from his creation.

Perhaps most fatefully, the attention of many religious people began to turn away from the surrounding wonders of the creation which the emerging sciences were just then opening up, fatally narrowing their understanding of their faith and their reality and the crucial link between the two. Was this not in effect an abdication of the comprehensive nature of the traditional religious world-view: the worship of the God of all truth, spanning both reason and faith? This loss of the intellectual high ground may have happened imperceptibly at the time, but it was surely a catastrophe of major proportions for the Christian faith as a whole.

Little by little a more matter-of-fact, literal view of biblical truth and of the human predicament gained ground, forgetting the sacred, impenetrable mystery of our existence and the power of the language of myth to articulate this to the heart. Thus emerged a modern Christianity affected by a surface rationalism but increasingly estranged from key elements in its own deep roots as well as its surrounding culture. The tip of this iceberg in time became known as fundamentalism, but to some degree this wider embattled, defensive stance has influenced the faith as a whole and arguably still does today.

Meanwhile the logic of this new reality became more and more relentless, as a picture emerged of a machine-like, fully determined universe. For some, God had become the watch-maker who had put it together, wound it up and then had, as it were, walked away, no longer concerned about the fate of what was after all a fully predetermined creation. It was not long before the very basis of human freedom itself began to be seen as quite possibly a delusion, and God himself, consigned now to a supernatural realm of his own, as an unnecessary hypothesis.

The sense of an overarching sacred presence faded as people started to see God as just another player in the resistance against the invincible march of reason and progress. God, for so long the ultimate source and guarantor of truth, astonishingly was now beginning to be seen as its arch-enemy. It was in this truly revolutionary atmosphere that atheism became a plausible world-view and started to really gain in popularity.

The divide between reason and faith had apparently become unbridgeable and by the mid-twentieth century the general public had arrived at a particularly confusing point. The celebrated school pupil's answer to a religious studies exam question ran like this: 'What is faith? Faith is trying very hard to believe something which you know to be untrue.' Perhaps Christian belief was by this time struggling under the weight of too many contradictory images.

This chapter concludes the major part of our voyage, since it brings the story back full circle to our own time and the point at which the book started. The question now is, What can Jesus' insight say to us today, to the dilemmas and challenges of our own time? The final section of the book addresses this question.

Part Five
Consequences

Part Five examines some key issues which this book raises for us in our new century. Chapter 16 lays out some of the more striking implications of Jesus' distinctive understanding of his God, and considers what this might say to us today, when ideas of God are no longer widely accepted without challenge. Chapter 17 then ponders the paradox of preserving a faith against the ravages of time, and suggests ways beyond the current state of exile and discomfort, ways of bringing a renewed faith back in among the whole people once again.

Chapter 18 consciously looks back over the book and in so doing tries to rebalance and reconnect Kingdom theology and salvation theology. Chapter 19 tries to reconnect a faith fit for tomorrow to the understanding we now have of our own nature and of our place in the creation. Chapter 20 then examines the potential relevance of Jesus to our future as a species, more specifically to the daunting challenges humanity will face in the rest of this century.

This book returns finally to a fundamental paradox under-lying modern Christian belief. Despite the high reverence which the churches give to Jesus, they often tend to see him as a largely theological figure, a figure with a strangely two-dimensional, somehow unconvincing humanity. The final chapter recalls the very distinctive, awkward human being whose extraordinary vision set this whole thing in motion, and asks what was the secret at the heart of his teaching, the authentic source of his authority.

An appendix explores the idea of trinity, its origins, how it has been differently understood in different times, and what it could possibly mean to people today.

Chapter 16
New Light on God

Abba and the Gods of Today

Woody Allen is in his kitchen making himself a sandwich, and someone on the TV is talking about Einstein and the phenomenon of uncertainty in modern quantum physics. The person on the TV quotes Einstein's objection to the very idea of uncertainty in the fabric of the created world, in his famous words: 'God does not play dice.' Woody emphatically agrees, waving the knife in the air. 'That's right! God does not play dice! God does not play dice!' Then a pause, his knife poised above his sandwich while he looks out of the window. 'Hide and seek maybe, but not dice!'

Two things seem to characterize the picture so many people have of God in modern times. First, he is just another player in the creation story, a 'being', supreme in some sense, yes, but still a center of consciousness in some way like you or me, who can decide whether to create the worlds or not. Second, this modern perception of God often seems oddly shy, as if in retreat from his creation and from ordinary human experience. He really does seem to be hiding, in contrast to the God people saw in past historical periods, who could act and speak with great power. Today God is no longer self-evident.

The previous chapter outlined some of the history of this most curious development whereby God, the magnificent, mysterious presence within the creation, simply faded from the human imagination. What we had left was something decidedly smaller, the 'God of the gaps', still useful for a while in order to account for those aspects of the creation which the sciences had not yet been able to explain on their own. Of course this God seemed to be in constant retreat as the sciences advanced! The sciences, moreover, were clear and rational and represented the future, making religious faith look like an irrational throwback, clinging to a dark and inferior past. Attitudes like this were influential for much of the twentieth century, and atheist authors like Richard Dawkins or A.C. Grayling still write in this vein today.

The thing about this modern caricature of God is that he has nothing to say on the big, intractable, ultimate questions which still surround us: the awe-inspiring mystery of our boundless creation and the enduring puzzle of the human heart. This altogether smaller figure, who is somehow an adversary of scientific method, is the God whom modern atheists don't believe in, and in a way they are quite right. This travesty of the idea of God is surely unworthy of anyone's belief.

The fact is that today we have inherited a confusing jumble of different images of God, rather like the different images we have of Jesus himself. For some people, God is still pictured as the 'emperor of the universe', a model taken from the political history of the classical period and arguably well past its sell-by date by now. This God is often pictured sitting on a throne; he is august and distant, often a war God reminiscent of the Greek god Zeus: the God with the thunderbolt, punishing the wrongdoer through his awesome, almighty power. This God, then, is about power and force.

A further image picked up in more modern times is the God of the early scientists, the watchmaker who designs and makes the world like an intricate machine. This had an early vogue in the seventeenth and eighteenth centuries, after the epic work of Isaac Newton had established the picture of a mechanical universe not unlike a gigantic clockwork machine. This engineer God, however, seems to have wound up his machine, set it in motion and then walked away, supremely indifferent to human fate and human welfare. He seems to be, if anything, even more distant than God the emperor.

More modern reformulations essentially continue a similar

logic. One view sees God as the communicator of information, for example in the genome (according to this view, the most fundamental ingredient in the universe is not matter but information). Another even more abstract view is that God is the source of a universe which is at one and the same time intelligible yet contingent. But these again are distant, cerebral views of God.

Some historians suggest that the western, Latin-speaking tradition within Christianity has tended to overstress rational attempts to define God or to prove his necessary existence, a kind of theological equivalent to squaring the circle – an idea whose plausibility for many people in modern times has simply worn thin. By contrast, it is claimed, elements within the Eastern Orthodox tradition do seem to be more aware of the dazzling sacredness and mystery of our infinite surrounding reality. This tradition seems to understand better the elementary futility of any rational quest to define or understand the source of all that is, the profound mystery of existence itself.

Jesus' vision cuts right across all this line of reasoning with the eye of a poet. This source of all that is, this profound mystery of existence, is in reality exquisitely close to every one of us. For Jesus, Abba is intimately concerned with the everyday experience of human life and its persistent quest for dignity, meaning and wholeness. This God is closer to us than we ourselves could imagine, closer than breathing, closer than consciousness itself. This God is actually inseparable from us, almost like a part of us which we had been unaware of.

It does seem to have been this healer's interest in the dynamics of transforming the heart which led him into a new landscape, an entirely new vision of this loving presence at work within all human experience. To believe in God (or not) is a modern idea. Jesus had recognized his God at a deep instinctive level, and his teaching was focused on one thing only: to enable us to know this particular vision of God in the same intimate way he did. Intuitively he sensed that this gave human beings a new dignity which swept away the pretensions of social divisions and hierarchies. This new vision could transform how people saw themselves. That was its point.

Ego and Its Antidote

Jesus' mature vision starts and finishes with the utter contrast between the Kingdom of Heaven and the kingdoms of this world, so God is everything that the kingdoms of this world are not. The implications of this central understanding are immense.

In his early period before his baptism, Jesus apparently starts with the traditional picture of the God of Israel, but then at some point he sees that power is a pivotal part of the human problem. God therefore has to be the very antithesis of human power, even benevolent human power. Suddenly he sees that this God is about generosity and liberation, not power and control. The kingdoms of this world appealed to the baser human instincts, including fear perhaps most of all, and were characterized by people asserting human ego. (I understand the term 'ego' not in its specifically Freudian sense, but in the more popular sense of that within us which is egotistic, the sense which you might call the me-me-me within us all.)

Seen against this, Jesus' vision of God was quite fundamentally ego-less, just like the great creation itself in fact. This meant that the models of God based on politics and power no longer really fitted. If the ego was at the heart of humanity's exile, an exile from its surrounding creation and from the source of its own fulfillment, and if God was like an antidote capable of saving humanity from this exile, then ego was the diametric opposite of whatever God was.

The logic of this insight is perhaps worth dwelling on for a moment. Since this God is precisely that which saves us from the consequences of our ego, his nature has to be its very opposite: a self-forgetting and self-abandoning nature whose generosity simply overwhelms any human scale. This God is continuously at work within each of us, and maybe it is in our unconscious depths that we can most vividly touch the life of this creative process within us. The exile of the conscious mind from the creation within and around us – couldn't this be the whole human problem in a nutshell? This God is precisely the opposite of all that. This represents a whole alternative vision of the creation, a creation which never sleeps and works from within all things. This is a presence so close to us that it anchors our very awareness of ourselves in a deeper level of reality, deeper than all our desires and hopes and fears.

Another consequence of this arresting new vision, at first sight odd but perfectly logical for an ego-less presence within us, is that it cannot change us without our consent. So this God within works not by fighting against the ego or by overwhelming it by sheer force and power, but by gently and patiently winning its allegiance, by bringing it willingly into the new inner Kingdom. With this kind of God, if we can speak of power at all, it's the liberating power which comes from recognizing truth within us. We are, after all, the species for whom truth matters supremely. This is why this God can reach everyone, creating through this power of truth a new hope for the powerless, a constantly recurring hope of liberation for all who are imprisoned.

What if we use the word 'God' to refer to this Reality, this truth, beauty and love, to which we do seem to owe such unmistakable allegiance, to which we are somehow attuned, this Reality which is so essential in fact to our sanity and our fulfillment? This would mean that God's power is of an utterly different nature from human power but one which is immeasurably stronger. You might say that you can't defeat this kind of power by shooting it in the head or by hanging it on a cross. But if 'God' is our name for the power of truth, it could also just as well be our name for the ubiquitous energy of the creation, the universal never-ceasing unsinkable creativity on all sides, which creates us new every day in a detail which surpasses our ability to grasp it. Can't we with a modicum of poetic license call this power in our creation the power of something like love, but with an exuberant, overwhelming generosity beyond the limits of conventional human love, enfolding us on all sides?

Of course life can deal us fierce blows and we all have moments too when we need to get rid of our anger, to curse the whole theater, the whole bloody circus, and say that it is full of sound and fury, signifying precisely nothing. True to our authentic human nature, we want sometimes to blame everyone and everything else. But what is this object of our anger, this God who doesn't give a damn, who could prevent suffering but for his own sweet reasons doesn't bother to do so? Is this anything more than just another fantasy, handy when we need something to curse at but scarcely worth any kind of serious belief?

The God Jesus saw is the power which can make us whole, can lead us into a life more abundant, can bring us to the completion of our nature that we are born searching for. The parable of the prodigal son says it all. When the son finally returns home, having learned a bitter and humiliating lesson, his old man runs out to meet him, and in the words of the story, he falls on his neck and kisses him! How could I not celebrate? he says. This son of mine was dead and is alive again; he was lost and is found. What could be more natural? That is Jesus' picture of God, all told in a vivid story from life, short-circuiting the objections of logical reasoning. With this God, the bottom line is: We are loved more than we can imagine.

This God is first and foremost about healing the human heart, a healing which can accompany us as we go through life day by day, bringing an intoxicating fullness to the experience of living. You end up at peace, with more energy, more the person you always could have been. People live addicted to security, their lives crippled by caution, a stalking fear at the back of their head drawing so much of the lifeblood out of their experience of life. The God of Jesus liberates you from all that.

How did Jesus put it? Drink water and you will be thirsty again. Drink this water and you will never be thirsty again, because it will well up within you for ever.

Chapter 17
Faith in Exile

'That's my tip, if you ever find yourself in trouble, cling to the wreckage!'
It was advice that I thought I'd been taking for most of my life.
John Mortimer

Clinging to the Wreckage

Some people point to the survival of the churches as a special sign of God's blessing and support. Perhaps this is at best a heavily ironic blessing, given the shameful intolerance and cruelty to the people of the older covenant which have punctuated the history of Christian Europe. These are, after all, the very people who perhaps could have expected a special tender consideration from their spiritual cousins. Still, in an old biblical tradition human failure has always been contrasted with God's faithfulness, the one a constant foil for the other, our despondency about events always balanced by the constant possibility of repentance and new beginnings.

Perhaps the really remarkable survival is that of Jesus' own teachings, written down and interpreted by early followers with their own particular motives and understandings, and then reinterpreted and finessed down the centuries in a very human mixture of sincerity and axe-grinding. Perhaps just as remarkable is the process whereby the texts were re-examined and set in context in more recent times by the painstaking and devoted work of yet another host of people, this time experts also with their own limitations and disagreements and particular understandings. Surely the re-emergence today of a distinctive, coherent, challenging teaching in the face of such mountainous difficulties is the survival that really matters. For even after all

173

that humanity has done to distort it and bury it, Jesus' Kingdom teaching has indeed survived and can still touch and transform the human heart. Who knows, it may yet rekindle hope for a more fully human future for all of us.

Yet centuries of church authority and a long fateful alliance with political establishments have projected the picture of a distant God who commands and of a stern Jesus who seems to be on the side of the big battalions. This particularly sad reversal of the original teaching has led to an overemphasis on guilt and unworthiness, a teaching which many people in our own time have angrily and understandably discarded. Meanwhile the very core of the teaching – the intimate presence of Abba in the heart – while still accepted as doctrine, is for most people today a pale shadow of the fierce, transforming experience it once was. As an example of finessing the original teaching almost to a vanishing point, is this record not simply calamitous?

Meanwhile the habitual reliance on authority has also helped to keep the expression of the faith in the concepts and termi-nology of a civilization long dead. This and the retention of the whole panoply of the old vanished 'supernatural' universe have merely added to a sense of sheer incredulity for so many in our society. In all this, has there not been a loss of vitality as well as credibility, and doesn't all this define a degree of exile within a surrounding culture?

Some might say that a degree of exile is precisely what you might expect in a society so preoccupied with consuming and having everything, which prizes the rewards of greed and violence so highly, and which pays so little attention to the eternal realities of human nature, wrapping itself instead in an absurd cocoon of consuming and possessions and frantic, non-stop entertainment. Some Christians do respond some of the time to these issues, but many others are also preoccupied with other issues like the intricate legalities of permissible intercommunion or the status of gay people within church life, issues which seem to mark them off from the world in which most of their neighbors live.

Historically, moreover, as the faith drew away in suspicion from the sciences and retreated into its own separate world, it seemed to have become more pessimistic about human nature and the inspiring potential of the great creator Holy Spirit acting through us. Instead of this it seemed to place its hope for the future increasingly in a supernatural intervention from outside, like a deus ex machina in the last act of the human drama, the only hope for an irretrievably fallen humanity. Leaving problems of credibility to one side, many people today see this faith as half in love with the past, rather than inspiring the rest of us with a lively hope for the future.

Jürgen Moltmann draws our attention to a fateful consequence of the preoccupation with the language, issues and mindsets of the past:

> In the past two centuries a Christian faith in God without hope for the future of the world has called forth a secular hope for the future of the world without faith in God. Should there now be a parting of the ways in history, in which faith aligns itself with the past, and unfaith with the future?[98]

In fact this faith appears to have set itself not only against the adversaries of the Kingdom, but against some of the key intellectual foundations of a whole society. Over the last few centuries has it not perhaps taken on too many unnecessary adversaries, too many to concentrate entirely effectively on the ones that matter?

It appears that the course of history itself has left us with an ironic contrast. On the one hand the teachings of Jesus, clarified and revived in our time by the efforts of so many people, may be able to speak to people again in the language of their own time. What is more, it can do this at a time in which this teaching could yet be vital. On the other hand public respect for the image of Jesus projected by the churches has sunk, significantly reducing the chances that his teaching will be taken seriously by enough people to make a difference. Isn't it time more church people woke up to the danger of this? Isn't there something not healthy in this seemingly permanent exile?

The Wholeness of Creation

We do seem to have finally left behind the long period in which the sciences seemed to be confidently dismissive of the validity of the religious quest. Today, as the awesome nature of our backdrop becomes clear, more scientists are aware of the wonder they are encountering and of the human need and the human instinct to respond to that wonder. Growing understanding of this may in time, who knows, build a new consensus on the future shape of religion in human affairs. Some authors predict a dynamic future for the major world religions in a longer perspective as they perforce encounter each other and together encounter the modern world.

At the same time the challenge from the sciences continues unabated. For example, there has recently been an upsurge of interest in consciousness and the relationship between body, brain and mind. 'Live' moment-by-moment brain mapping, ever more detailed understanding of the biochemistry of emotions and perception, and other concurrent advances are attracting the thoughtful attention of evolutionary psychologists, philosophers, neuroscientists and people from a whole range of other disciplines. One upshot of this is that people are challenging the long-held assumption that the mind, and with it all religious experience, as a subjective phenomenon must remain beyond scientific investigation, a fortress forever safe from attack. The nature of consciousness itself is now a topic of intense investigation.

This is an exciting development, but in itself hardly an attack on Jesus' Kingdom teaching, probably more of a challenge to much of Christianity's classical and medieval luggage, the elaborations of later centuries. The teaching about Abba and our generous, overwhelming creation, about the presence of a Holy Spirit dynamically at work within everyone in an inborn Kingdom in the human heart – this teaching need have no real quarrel with the sciences. In fact this minimal core gospel seems to be pretty much at ease in today's culture. It's not just that it asserts nothing which might create discord with the world of the sciences; it can also find deep inspiration once again in the endless wonders of the creation, following the inspiration Jesus himself took from the natural world he knew in his time.

For some time now, many Christians in different traditions have been paying more attention to this Kingdom teaching, the core teaching of the author of their faith, putting it back closer to the heart of how they understand their faith today. Perhaps this can help this historic faith at last to come out of its long cultural cul-de-sac. There are reasons for hope, if not for easy optimism. The one thing we can be confident about is that the workings of the Holy Spirit within the human heart will be as creative and as unpredictable as ever. We can expect surprises.

Once again people are beginning to appreciate the splendor and the unity of the creation, and the sacredness of their own place in it. People can see that the conflict between faith and the sciences has been a tragedy with fairly devastating consequences and a needlessly dispiriting burden. Freed from this burden, people can now work at the exciting task of renewing their understanding of this faith for their own time, making it vibrate once again with a living hope expressed in the language of the times. Perhaps if they have the courage to take this leap of trust, the future of the churches may actually turn out brighter than it has been for these past few centuries. Above all, if the faith feels more confident from within, its trust in its God will seem less beleaguered and more natural, and people will notice the change. The God of surprises will have come back among the whole people again. Under the surface there is a resilience in this tradition.

If we look back over the last 2,000 years, it can seem hard to envisage a faith free of the hierarchical, authority-based attitudes which have characterized it and confused its message for so much of the time up to now. But if we imagine future millennia stretching ahead of us, it may yet turn out that these first two will be seen as no more than a preliminary period. Maybe we have still to see the true flowering of the Kingdom teaching, finally unencumbered by the trappings and attitudes of this faith's long early marriage to political power.

According to a recent report in the *New Scientist*, evolutionary biologists have taken an interest in the possible evolutionary advantages of religious belief, arguing that creatures with some kind of systematic, reasoned hope in the future will stand a better chance of surviving dangerous times.[99] Psychological studies have established apparently that people with a religious belief are more contented, live longer, suffer fewer physical and mental illnesses, and even recover faster from surgical interventions, than people who have no such beliefs. There are even suggestions that humans may be in some degree hard-wired for transcendence. These findings should probably be treated with caution, but they do remind us that we are made to make sense of things, that truth and reality matter to us, that we do respond to the mystery and the grandeur which we encounter through all things.

The Scottish philosopher and theologian T.F. Torrance, long preoccupied with both the Trinity and the whole project of the sciences, came to see a renewed Trinitarian theology as a bridge, a way of holding the middle ground between the objective world of the sciences and an introverted postmodern culture obsessively circling around the individual's subjective experience – the age-old problem of the human ego in another guise.[100] He drew parallels between theological and scientific quests for truth, even describing the scientist as a high priest of the creation!

This appellation may yet prove less outlandish than it sounds at first hearing. It may yet be our awesome creation which can lead us beyond the fear, greed and loneliness which present culture generates. As we awake once again in our own time to the overwhelming glory of this creation, this may yet give us a leading hint to our own destiny as a species. The science writer Brian Swimme predicts that the destiny of humanity is not power and control, nor an endless round of acquisition and consuming, but, in his word, enchantment.[101] Who knows, a world culture of creativity and wonder, community and celebration may be around the next few corners, not as far away as we think. (Goethe, after a lifetime spanning literature, philosophy and science, concluded, '*Zum Erstaunen bin ich da*' – 'I am here in order to wonder.')

Some scientists today have been distancing themselves from the certainties of the machine model of the universe which so influenced thinking during the last two centuries. The universe which we now encounter has more of the awesome mystery, the sense of something which encompasses us, which is familiar to theologians. An appreciation of the wonder of that surrounding reality which has given us birth could yet be a bridge in the way that Torrance understood it, a bridge joining two sides to our human nature which in recent centuries have become alienated from one another.

This bridge could lead us into one quest, one grail, the definitive human quest to encounter that reality, both the inner and the outer, to grapple with it and to come to terms with it, in short to know it and, in the process of doing so, to finally come to know ourselves.

Chapter 18
When All is Said and Done

Fault Lines and Fundamentals

This book has explored some problems associated with this strange exile from contemporary culture which seems to have afflicted the Christian faith in recent centuries. It has tried to put the language of miracle and the supernatural into historical perspective in today's mysterious rational universe of continuous miracle. It has argued that the image of a stern, disapproving, morally cold Jesus reflects church doctrinal authority gone badly wrong, far removed from the Jesus of the narrative Gospels. It has tried to draw the picture, from these same Gospels, of one man's understanding undergoing a remarkable maturing process in which it finally achieved a depth of analysis and a personal challenge to his fellow humans which may be quite possibly unique in any civilization.

However, the book has also identified several sources of common incredulity which do seem to be built into this picture. One is the cultural strangeness of some aspects of Jesus' thinking and the difficulty of making any kind of sense of them for people today. How, for example, can we really understand his motivation for challenging the Roman authority in the way he did? Try as we may, it is hard for us to enter imaginatively into his culture or to make straightforward sense of this today, and this may for some people undermine the credibility of the rest of his teaching.

A further problem we looked at is that for many people today the picture of Jesus is just too strongly associated with a more traditional image taught and projected by the churches, and they simply cannot manage to free themselves from it. Some Christians just want to hold onto the picture they believe in, and some atheists want to hold onto the same picture precisely because they don't believe in it – both presumably drawing comfort from it, but for opposite reasons.

Another problem goes deeper. Jesus' teaching anticipates the natural defensive reactions inside the human heart when it is challenged to face up to its own motives. In fact, his challenge to us can get right underneath our defenses, right down to a tender point within us. Some people will find this very achievement the most convincing thing about it. Others, made skeptical by hard experience, may be angered by what they see as its naive optimism, while others again may even find it invasive or threatening and may instinctively want to have nothing to do with it.

Earlier in the book a fault line in very early Christianity was identified, between the Jewish inspiration of Jesus' pre-crucifixion teachings on the one hand, and on the other hand the interpretations made on the events surrounding and following the crucifixion itself, often by people more influenced by the surrounding Greek culture. All four narrative Gospels are candid witnesses to this fault line, each of them giving extended attention to both overarching themes – the teaching and the passion story – and trying to find a logic with which to connect them.

In a strange way there may be a similarity between the time in which the four Gospel narratives were written and our own time today. In the late first century there was a danger of a largely unreal, cosmic, god-like figure crowding out the memory of Jesus as a real human being. That may be one reason why the evangelists went out of their way to include so many telling human details of him in their accounts. Our view today is not their view, but we too have a similar need, do we not, to counteract a largely unreal view of Jesus? Don't we in our own time need to rediscover his full humanity once again? I hope that this book has conveyed something of this to the reader. (The portrait of Jesus will be completed in the final chapter.)

Something resembling the aforesaid fault line has survived recognizably right into modern times. Those who focus on the Kingdom teaching as the foundation of the faith, as this book does, can face a degree of challenge in explaining the meaning of the passion events. I hope that the detailed meditation on the story of the passion in Chapters 11 and 12 of this book represents a thoughtful response to this problem. As the book argues, the passion events can be understood as a dramatization of the teaching. Here is the self-forgetting, self-giving God envisioned in the teaching, now enacted in this extraordinary human drama, allowing this vision to penetrate below the radar of our resistance mechanisms and move the heart.

However, those for whom the events of the passion express the essential core of the faith run an opposite risk. If it is Jesus' death and resurrection which saves us and if all we have to do is believe in it, then we may underrate the full meaning of this remarkable teaching. This is perhaps a more serious charge, and many Christian churches have arguably done just this to some degree throughout history. You could say that they have made Christianity into a faith *about* Jesus rather than the faith *of* Jesus as expressed in his teaching. At its worst this can produce a reduced, handy-size, user-friendly version of a faith, largely stripped of the logic of its appeal to the human heart. It could be an important challenge for Christians today and tomorrow to reconnect these two halves of their faith more convincingly, and to find a more integrated way of understanding and expressing both sides: the Kingdom teaching and the passion story.

The teaching about our inner Kingdom has its own internal coherence and its own appeal to the heart. It is complete in itself. By contrast, although it may sound strange to say so, the passion events – however you interpret them – do not really stand on their own in this way but may be read as a dramatization of the teaching which preceded them.

This book revisited this teaching, identifying what some

might call lost or forgotten fundamentals within it. One example is the absoluteness of the contrast between the Kingdom of Heaven within us and the ways of a competitive, hierarchical, often violent world devoted to greed and power. Another is the lethal danger of the love of money and its ever-present capacity to distract us and, in the end, rob us of our birthright as children of this inner Kingdom. A further core teaching is the gentle spirit of love and respect for ourselves and for all our fellow humans, be they good or bad, friend or foe. Fitting in with these, almost like the center pieces in a jigsaw, are Jesus' nature teachings, familiar to many people today but almost as incidental asides. It is the nature teachings, after all, which justify the relationship of trust at the heart of the Kingdom teaching – it's the overwhelming generosity of the creation around us which witnesses to the self-giving love of our creator, as Jesus saw it. And it is this in turn which endows humanity with its new high status and dignity.

On reflection it may be too much to call these teachings lost fundamentals; perhaps they're not entirely lost, but their centrality in the logic of the Kingdom seems to have been blurred over. The point of one or two of them has become a bit vague perhaps and some have been radically misunderstood, like the celebrated teaching on turning the other cheek, discussed in Chapter 9. It's as if the Kingdom teaching has become an optional extra for those select few people who have a special calling for holiness. Now that really would be a serious distortion of the original teaching!

At this point I'd like to compare two situations and let you, the reader, judge them for yourself. First, Jesus' Kingdom teaching offers us an analysis of the human condition and a call for radical change which can ring true for us but can also come up against a force within us which resists this call to change. Perhaps it's our inner uncertainty at the radical nature of the challenge we are being faced with which causes us to hesitate. At one level our hesitation is perfectly understandable but it is nevertheless quite likely to keep our exuberant inner Kingdom from coming alive in our experience.

Second, there is the situation of the Christian faith itself in the last few centuries, unsure of the challenge of radical change, resisting the need to abandon positions of authority in a new kind of dialogue with the sciences and surrounding culture, and afraid of the unpredictable consequences of doing so. Perhaps a similar mixture of human motives is behind the resistance of the churches to accepting this particular challenge. In both situations perhaps we need courage to embrace change and really come alive. It's all very understandable. We want to make this leap of trust but we can't quite bring ourselves to do it! How very human!

Choices and Responses

This book, then, presents the reader with some choices. You can choose to believe both the teaching and the later doctrine, if you can tolerate the degree of tension between them which can arise. Some people will find this easier than others. Alternatively you can choose initially to believe just the teachings – the proclamation of the Kingdom within us all – seeing this as enough in itself. You can then take a more skeptical line with any of the later doctrines whenever they seem to dilute or distort this teaching. You could call this Kingdom-centered Christianity, and this book argues that this view may be clearer and simpler, perhaps a particular priority these days.

There again, you can choose to keep a certain distance from the whole thing, both the teachings and the later doctrines. Maybe the Christian faith for you has drifted too far from the world you know, leaving it culturally too strange to be fully credible or trustworthy. Or quite possibly you may have other reservations which I cannot even guess at.

The one remaining option is to believe the later doctrine of the churches and in effect to use these doctrines as a yardstick to judge the teaching of the founder. You might recognize in this picture a bit of a caricature of one or two churches today, and it must be said that some weighty theologians have come pretty close to this view. I would suggest that this option is simply upside down. The pre-crucifixion teachings are surely the fountain from which everything else flows, both historically and theologically.

It is worth underlining twice over, however, that the emphasis in this book on a Kingdom-centered Christian faith need not be seen as an alternative or a rival to a salvation-centered faith. Many people will find it perfectly possible to keep these two ways of understanding Christianity in harmony. Different people will lay more stress on one or the other.

What this book does argue is that Jesus' Kingdom teaching stands on its own as a unique understanding of the human condition. It offers us a way out of the meaningless round of futile ego-enslavement, it liberates us from the prison house of the self, and it heals the fear-laden sickness of the heart which accompanies this condition like a shadow. It saves us from all this. The idea of salvation, then, can be understood as an expression or summary of this Kingdom teaching, dramatized in the passion events.

Whatever your reaction to all this, I hope that this portrait of Jesus has come out at least clear, fresh and alive. I hope that it has rescued a believable, human picture of Jesus from the shadowy, two-dimensional figure worshipped in many churches today and the altogether incredible travesty of him which still survives in the public imagination more widely.

It's the human logic of Jesus' teaching that in the end convinces me. While I have been engaged in a quest to make sense of him, I suddenly realize that he has made sense of me. He teaches me to calm down, to accept life as a great gift, and to take a more skeptical but also affectionate look at my own relentless ego. He dares me to stop holding onto things and to start giving myself away to the people around me. He persuades me to love life extravagantly, without any barriers, with all my heart and all my mind and all my soul, every morning when I wake.

Now I can look in the mirror, see myself with new eyes, and smile back at what I see with compassion and with real affection. I once was blind, but now I see.

Chapter 19
Agenda: Reclaiming Ourselves

Although it is part of my nature, I cannot understand all that I am. This means, then, that the mind is too narrow to contain itself entirely. But where is that part of it which it does not itself contain?
Augustine of Hippo

The Logic of Complexity

Jesus makes a distinctive sense of us. He comes up with a sophisticated picture of us in our very human complexity, with our intelligence and our insecurity somehow linked, distracted by surface passions yet intuiting deeper wisdom underneath the surface of experience. Childhood memories haunt us, just possibly both the cause and the cure for our condition.

He pictures us, not in our customary social context but simply as creatures of an overwhelmingly generous creation, and he uses the intimate language of childhood to give to us a wholly new dignity and truly royal status as adored children of a parent-like creator. This great leap of the imagination really can move mountains. Our complexity creates a perpetual dynamic of experience and choice, failure and recovery, suffering and rebirth, a drama of continuing inner dialogue with a mysterious creator alive within our own depths, a drama set against the mystery and grandeur of our creation itself. This picture is radical, challenging, hopeful, and surely worth our attention in our own century. How does this picture match what we know about human nature today?

We now know that even the most ordinary experiences of everyday living rest on the surface of unimaginably complex foundations. As creatures, products of the indescribable process of the evolution of life on this planet, we are infinitely more special than we commonly imagine we are. It is hardly surprising, though, that our conscious mind with its limited attention span seems to have such difficulty in deciphering itself, and perhaps this is what generates the deep undertow of anxiety within us which we surely all share to some degree. Perhaps this is the beginning of our restless search for a key to life.

But maybe we underrate ourselves. By the very same token, precisely because of our deeply complex creativity, human beings maybe *can* eventually arrive at a vision which cuts through the confusion and the fear, despite the daunting nature of the task on first examination. Jesus' transforming vision of our inner Kingdom does just this, does it not? It understands not only the underlying anxieties arising out of our complexity but the possibilities in our dynamic creativity as well. Change the vision, and maybe we can change ourselves after all.

Maybe this vision is not quite as unrealistic as it seems to be at first glance. It's true that, within us, various mechanisms do their best to protect us and in their own way to look after our welfare. This book outlined some of these in an earlier chapter. The unconscious mechanism which selects what we give our attention to, which in effect selects what we see, was one example. The mechanism to project responsibility out from ourselves onto other people was another. But at the same time the human species is distinguished by its prodigious ability to learn from experience and to reflect deeply and creatively on that experience. Instinctively, at its deepest level, it is programmed to seek and create sense, pattern, meaning, reality – and it will keep trying to do this even against the odds.

In the teaching of the two contrasting kingdoms, Jesus gives us an entirely new perspective, a template through which we can suddenly see new patterns and realities, and this experience of breaking through our doubts can feel like a true moment of discovery. Perhaps the internal agent of this discovery, which Christians refer to as the Holy Spirit, works within us in much the same way as the other internal mechanisms, only it taps deeper levels. Perhaps it can finally clarify and unify the contra-dictory jungle of the human heart with all its conflicting emotions and resistance mechanisms.

In this new Kingdom of Heaven we are children of a creation whose energy and glory out-scale us at every point, yet we are alive with its life, in ourselves reflecting the full glory of the whole thing. Its awe-inspiring glory is the true source of our value; the stunning intricacy of our bodies, and even more so of our brains, is its gift to us. Much of the time we will forget its presence but we are enfolded in it. It is part of us; it is part of how we are created. This vision can give us a new sense of our own inherent value, a value not from social status or from our own strenuous efforts but from our natural state as creatures of this indescribable creation. This can fill us with renewed energy, enthusiasm, exhilaration – strength enough to follow this teacher into the living Kingdom of Heaven, new every day.

These days, we are in any case learning to see new visions of ourselves all the time. For example, it's only in comparatively recent times that we have come to understand that we are part of the infinitely fragile biosphere, an exquisite film of life on the surface of our small, jewel-like planet. Likewise in recent times we are beginning to see ourselves as citizens of one world community. New visions characterize the age we live in. If we can now in a similar way learn to see through the fear inside us, and the craving, and the greed, and the lust for power, and the futility of all that, and if we can see clearly our true worth, our true beauty – if we can achieve all of that, who can say what we cannot go on to achieve?

Scientists today are used to the idea of stable systems which for a time resist change until they reach a tipping point, and then quite suddenly they can change into something which behaves quite differently and more appropriately to the new situation. Could the human race be in the process of undergoing this kind of process, awaiting the moment of transformation? Perhaps the potential to create miracles is there, dormant inside each of us.

So is the future bright? The near future might quite possibly turn out to be every bit as ghastly as that comprehensive calamity, the first half of the twentieth century. Thoughtful pessimists are still warning of the real possibility of a truly apocalyptic future for all of us.[102] So where can we discern reasons for hope? A central feature of human nature seems to be a continuous dialogue between an array of inner defense mechanisms and a deeper-set instinct to integrate these with a wider, farther-seeing wisdom. Characteristically this dialogue takes time to resolve, and it may take a disaster or two to really make us concentrate and learn key lessons. Time and again human history is a case of two steps forward and one step back.

In Jesus' Kingdom of Heaven we are given reason to hope in defiance of surrounding darkness. Victory is not guaranteed; we have to fight for it. It takes commitment, and this too is part of how we are.

Adult and Child

When it comes down to it, isn't the contradiction at the heart of human nature the fact that we live out a persistent delusion, namely that the point of living is to maximize our own comfort and advantage, as if each of us were the center of our own little universe? This is built into us, and time after time we find ourselves slipping back into it like a default mode, but it leaves us cloyed and imprisoned within ourselves. Intuitively we sense that there is a larger reality out beyond this prison, which can seem pretty scary so long as we stay safe inside, but we also sense that this larger reality can be more exciting and in the end more fulfilling. Perhaps the adventure of truth really can set us free.

In the end our human destiny has to include some journey from ignorance to understanding, does it not? This can be characteristically a journey from fear of fear itself to a managed and understood fear, a journey which is capable of producing in us a cool courage, as if from nowhere. Of course it's human too to reject the challenge, to bolt like a young horse out of its stall in sheer unacknowledged funk. But sooner or later maybe it isn't too much to hope that human beings will start to find it fashionable to know themselves, find it cool to cut the bluster and self-deception and acknowledge their fears, to learn to really open up to themselves and live more adventurously. Decidedly cooler than living out much of our life in fearful ignorance, our existence grey with uncertainty, crippled by an angry frustration and a relentless need for security.

This shift of our center of gravity out from this imprisoning ego to the whole creation, creating space for wonder and trust at the heart of daily living, can feel like liberating new dimensions within ourselves which all this time had been tied up. And entering this new Kingdom can indeed feel like becoming a little child again, summoning up our courage for the adventure, liberating the child within us, as Jesus saw all those centuries ago. Becoming like a little child does seem to be central to his vision. It's the complement to the experience of Abba, of God as an essentially parental presence; the one fits the other quite closely. Nor is this just an idea which we can contemplate and perhaps admire or critically examine. Jesus says we can enter this Kingdom of the heart only if we become as little children in our relationship to this intimate presence within, this Abba. It's about opening up to this overarching reality and daring to give our whole trust to the whole experience of living.

It's so easy to forget what we are: creatures, just that. And although we sometimes behave like overconfident, under-experienced children (the other side of childhood), acting as if we owned the place, at other times we can see through this behavior, seeing its childlike absurdity. Perhaps it's not just that we *should* be as little children; perhaps this is telling us that in some ways we *are* little children, but we don't like to admit it to ourselves.

Becoming as little children, then, can be like coming home to reality, seeing ourselves as we really are: stumbling around in the dark, whistling loudly to drive away the uncertainty at the back of our heads, yet, all the while, princesses and princes of this dazzling creation. Yes, at first sight this uncompromising level of honesty seems an uncomfortable place to be, perhaps putting our defense mechanisms on orange alert the moment we consider it. But the beauty of the vision of the Kingdom of Heaven is precisely that we can look in the mirror and see ourselves truly for the first time, as the very energy and glory of the great creation itself shines back at us through our own eyes.

More than this, since we are anchored in the reality of this creation, as its true children, it can dawn on us that the very human fear that we are irretrievably alone is in reality a delusion. Today different fields of study like psychology and biology document the many ways in which we are indeed indissolubly bound to our creation, defined in fact by our manifold links with it. And once we have understood this, nothing can ever again take it away from us. Nothing can ever separate us from it. We can walk tall, proud of our new status. We can hold our heads up high!

This maybe all sounds too good to be true, and we start looking for the catch, and the catch may be precisely that we can't quite bring ourselves to take this leap of trust. At this point it's as if Jesus says, OK, don't jump if it feels wrong, but keep it in mind; don't dismiss it out of hand just yet. But meanwhile do notice the consequences of jumping and of not jumping. Quite simply, we have a choice. If we carry on cultivating and hiding behind our ego, the feeling of alone-ness might very well return to dog us.

Yet we can learn to see through the ego, this tyrant with its futile self-centeredness. We can learn little by little to actually give ourselves away, and to cultivate a new kind of uninhibited love for our neighbor and for the whole shooting match. If we take this risk, then we might find ourselves at a point where we have forgotten to be alone. As the children's song puts it,

> Love is something if you give it away,
> You end up having more.[103]

And we would be responding to our creation in admiring imitation, opening ourselves to it, or in the more traditional Christian words, we would be learning to love God because he first loved us.

But this message is not just for the likes of you or me; it's for all humankind. So perhaps this book needs to end, not with one individual caught in the present moment, but with all of us, the whole human race, turning our thoughts forward to our joint future. That is where the challenge lies, and the hope, and the apprehension.

Chapter 20
Agenda: Reclaiming the Future

Jesus' teaching of a Kingdom of Heaven gives us a new perspective within which to see ourselves and what we might be able to achieve. It promises us that we can become more whole, more complete, calming our habitual fears and doubts. It speaks of a source of strength and creativity deep within us which can give us new energy as individuals and as a whole civilization. There is a universal quality to this which can speak in any age, and I think it speaks to us with a peculiar force in our age too, an age characterized by looming challenges, soaring new aspirations and ancient fears.

Within Christianity there have always been two views of the future dimension of the Kingdom teaching. One tradition believes that at some future time in the human story this Kingdom of love and trust really will break through into politics and transform human life on earth. Human beings really will have learned to change their behavior in crucial ways. Another tradition takes a more pessimistic view of our nature, believing that human perfectibility will always remain a dream continually put off into the future, always a judgment on our incorrigible ways. There is a real and long-running tension between these two interpretations.

This tension has resurfaced in modern times, perhaps especially after the devastation of two world wars and the unspeakable events which took place in their wake. Will the human race finally learn wisdom, recognize the source of its true fulfillment and manage to survive? Hope and despair are still finely balanced, but perhaps the onus is on those who can still hope to establish credible grounds for this hope. Fortunately, new emerging understanding is converging today from different quarters, and this may help build a reasonable case for hope.

History through a Telescope

In recent years the emerging subject of human prehistory has been quietly transforming the historical perspective within which we understand ourselves, studying as it does the evolution of our human ancestors and their prehuman predecessors, at the frontier between history and biology. The date of the very earliest cities is being pushed back to 6,000, 8,000, some say even 10,000 years ago. Going back further, evidence of art, decorative objects, ceremony, worship and the sacred date back to anything between 30,000 and 50,000 years ago. Modern humans apparently emigrated out of their African homeland somewhere around 60,000 to 100,000 years ago – estimates of this vary widely.[104] Our ancestors, anatomically modern humans, were around in Africa for many tens of thousands of years before that.

In our first 100,000 years or so, there may very well have been a degree of routine but relatively small-scale local violence, but human life was nevertheless very different from today – much more a matter of isolated small groups in loose alliances over great stretches of land. Conflict would have often led to further migration into still empty land, rather than to large-scale slaughter. Seen in this perspective, it is now possible to see the more recent past – the last 8,000 to 10,000 years, say – as transitional, characterized by increasing crowding, competition, greed, patriarchy, empires and war. One might even compare this to an adolescent phase in human development. Is it also possible that the present twenty-first century crisis is signaling the end of this transitional phase and the final emergence of a single world community? There are reasons to hope so.

A Fork in the Road

Today we live in interesting times. We are witnesses to the early stages of a process in which the world really does seem to be coming together for the first time as one community. In Moltmann's striking words:

> In the past human beings had histories in the plural but no common history in the singular. Today we have pasts in the plural; each people, each culture, each religion has its own past. But since in the future we will either perish together or survive in a new community, we have a future only in the singular. We have many pasts but only one future.[105]

For just over half a century we have had in the United Nations, with all its current limitations, what is already recognizably a world legislature and civil service, and now much more recently we have even seen the hesitant beginnings of a functioning world criminal court. Ever so gradually, law is beginning to replace might, and a process similar to individual nation building may be at last stuttering to life on a worldwide scale.

The consequences of war today are apparently becoming more complicated and burdensome, and this may be acting as a brake on those who are contemplating starting one. Already, aggressive wars are being seen more widely as economically and ecologically ruinous to both sides. In addition, life is becoming legally risky to those who may have charges of crimes against humanity laid against them – political leaders are now less safe from legal arrest outside their own borders. More and more legal cases are being brought by citizens among a target population, for murder and restitution of damage, and by an army's own soldiers for mental and physical injuries. Life is never straight-forward, but the world may be in transition from a lawless condition like the old Wild West to something more like a normal law-abiding community.

In world trade economics, too, a growing sense of mutual interdependence between major world economies in an increas-ingly multipolar world may help to dampen enthusiasm for military options. The world economic crisis of 2008 illustrates this dramatically – in an internationalized stock market a disturbance anywhere is soon felt everywhere. Yet we are still stuck with a world economics system designed to serve an apparently limitless human capacity for greed, presiding over behavior which could still seriously damage the fragile balance of the earth on which all living things depend. This, too, is slowly becoming better understood.

Some people put their trust in technology. But as we watch the two Asian giants emerging as proudly affluent societies, their economies roughly doubling in size every decade, it is hard to see how technology on its own could ever solve our problem of long-term survival. Looking ahead, even the audacious geo-engineering technologies, which promise to slow down global warming, at best might just buy us a decade or two more time, merely postponing the human crisis. It may be slowly dawning on us that humanity really does seem to be approaching an important fork in the road and that quite possibly some of our traditional assumptions and ways of doing politics are just not going to be very useful to us for much longer. Like oil, their days may be numbered. Academic attention is now turning to the problem of excessive, often mindless consumption in rich economies. (One such academic endeavor is the Millennium Assessment of Human Behavior, a forum set up at Stanford University for global discussion of related ethical and cultural issues.[106])

Two futures seem to be beckoning to us: one of serial calamities and increasingly violent conflict, the other of a new age of prosperity and cooperation amid a new sense of a single world community of interests. In practice, quite possibly we may end up for a time oscillating between these scenarios. But if the latter option is to become a securely sustainable reality, it does look as if the human species will have to change the way it sees itself, the way it understands its own needs, and therefore the way people need to behave, both individually and globally. As far as we can see, things will have to start moving really seriously within the next 20 years, as the two polar ice caps retreat year by year and the glaciers shrink on all the high mountain ranges. Some would argue for a greater urgency than this. By now, at least in the West, a mass audience is becoming alarmed.

In fact if we are to survive as a species, as a new worldwide community, it begins to look as if a whole attitude change on a worldwide scale may be required of us. So, alongside developing new technologies, it does seem only a matter of time before we will have to dig deeper, to re-examine the human behavior in whose interests all this technology is to be employed. Can we convince people that they maybe no longer need today's high levels of relentless consumption, and that the associated need for a fortress mentality in our approach to world security may be making it too dangerous in any case? Perhaps a more robust skepticism towards today's high levels of affluence may become fashionable within the lifetime of some of us alive today, provided that people are given a credible alternative. The present world of greed and fear and violence has simply made current lifestyles too dangerous, too big a menace to all our futures.

On a global level we seem to be focusing so much of our efforts on creating wealth and raising our standard of living. But this may be pouring oil on the fire. Wealth creates its own surreal addictions and sooner or later stokes the fires of greed, and fear and violence are seldom far behind. This is a familiar treadmill, is it not? And Jesus speaks to it directly. He shows us a different perspective within which to understand ourselves and whatever it is that drives us. Once people see themselves in new ways, old preferences for confrontation and mindless consumption may in time come to seem pointless, an empty treadmill going nowhere.

Jesus works over the whole area of human nature and human

need at a quite unusual depth. In his teaching of the inner Kingdom we truly can see ourselves in new ways. This teaching, moreover, shows us ourselves in the context of our whole creation, not just that of our human social context. Jesus' teaching can also open us up to our own unconscious, with its layered dynamic, its resistance mechanisms, and its underlying search for a key to living. So this teaching opens us up beyond our social context in both directions at once: to our own unconscious and to our whole creation.

If human nature were indeed incorrigibly greedy and incapable of learning anything better, then we really would be in a deep hole, but in serious emergencies in the past humans have managed to change quite radically, provided they could see what needed to be done and why it was worth doing. And if we can do that, perhaps we may come across ways of doing more than just survive. Perhaps we will find ways of thriving together in a new consensus, creating a new civilization of discovery and creativity in which we can truly cherish our wonderful planet.

We do seem to have two generic instincts. On the one hand we have an instinct to fall back into a kind of default mode, which makes us go for our own comfort and advantage, as if each of us was entirely alone in the world. On the other hand, in moments of clarity we can see that this isn't enough, that in fact it is inherently unstable. We have the instinct to keep searching for the key to something which is more likely to satisfy us permanently. Deep inside us, we know perfectly well that there is more to the real treasure of life than our standard of living.

What we seem to need is a new vision of ourselves which shows us a way beyond this default mode, an altogether larger vision of ourselves and our deepest needs. If this larger self-understanding can then break out into politics worldwide, this may give us reason to hope that we can survive after all. This is certainly nail-bitingly uncertain, but a glimmer of hope does hang on, despite everything, even if it does seem at times that hope is about all we have left. Besides, hope may be converging from another quarter.

A New Heaven and a New Earth

Another entirely new vision of ourselves is in any case already coming to us from the strange, awesome new world which the sciences have uncovered in the past half-century. This might seem at first sight to be an irrelevant distraction, but it might be in fact very timely because it could reinforce a new human self-understanding which may be just emerging.

Remember that Jesus' Kingdom teaching places us in the context of our whole creation. Today we are just beginning to take in just how endlessly wonderful our surrounding universe is. Some of the explanations offered by the sciences in parts of this new world may at first glance seem startling, even unlikely, especially perhaps to someone who is encountering it all for the first time, as many people are. The sheer scale of the creation alone may seem implausible to untutored eyes, for example to someone who is not used to the idea that as we look out into the night sky we are looking back in time, such is the unimaginable scale of what we are encountering. At this stupendous scale, time and space seem to be eerily interwoven.

Awesome levels of deep complexity, moreover, appear on all sides wherever we look, right through the fabric of our universe, even within the very atoms and molecules from which the material world, and all of us, are made. But we encounter this deep complexity at the level of human experience too. A truly awesome complexity lies in the cascade of chemical reactions within the brain of the peregrine falcon as, with an exquisite instantaneous tilt of her wings and head, she adjusts angle and velocity and accelerates into the final swoop. Meanwhile her every move is caught in the binoculars of the boy lying in the marram grass, and an answering fountain cascade of chemicals sweeps through his brain in turn, as he shivers with breathless admiration at the secret beauty which he has just witnessed.

This new world can be humbling but can also inspire us in ways which we are unlikely to forget. These perfectly everyday wonders are effortlessly matched on a very much larger scale again, as we witness the size and power and dynamics of two galaxies gracefully smashing into one another in the glacial slow motion of a multi-million-year-long collision. This is tracked by these intriguing new primates recently evolved on the little blue planet somewhere in the depths between Sagittarius and Orion. By now, the old, limited machine-model of the universe has long since flown out of the window, as incredible as the old emperor-model of God.

But it can really send a shiver down the spine when it dawns on us that the awesome power of this strange and inspiring creation also lies deep within us. We are made, as they say, of stardust, made with exquisite design out of the elements cooked in the nuclear fires inside innumerable stars over billions of years. When this finally sinks in, it can make us more thoughtful, indeed skeptical, but also more alert to it as *our* creation, more willing to be thankful for its great gift to us, and more energized and creative in our efforts to see that we and our children survive within it. Seen in the light of this new understanding, the issue of the survival of future generations as future witnesses of such marvels now has a new urgency, does it not?

Homo Sapiens

Current evolutionary thinking reminds us that change is not only possible but unavoidable and ubiquitous throughout nature, yet it takes place normally at an imperceptible pace, often compared with the pace of geological change over many millions of years. On this scale, humanity is a very new arrival, and its acquisition of language and intelligent thought has been so dramatically and rapidly successful that perhaps the very speed of this success has in a sense become the problem. It is alleged that the processes of evolution cannot cope with change happening at such breakneck pace and that the human experiment may therefore be doomed at the last to failure.

However, evolutionary thinking also allows for long periods of stability punctured by short periods of very rapid evolution due to special circumstances, and this may indeed be responsible for some of the major developments in evolution which have gone to make up today's natural world. Evidently our own emergence appears to have been one remarkable example of this extremely radical, rapid change. So perhaps we can survive after all. The leopard assuredly cannot change its spots within such a short span of time, and we are similarly unlikely to be able to change many of our more basic instincts in this time span either. Luckily, however, it seems we may be able to change our ways of behaving as opposed to changing those of our instincts, which are largely fixed. So presumably, we will continue to fall for delusory temptations, and will still have to learn wisdom (or not) from our own experience, from trial, error and reflection. We will still, in Mother Julian's sense, stumble, feel the pain, and dust ourselves down again.

Evolution famously works, not by going back to the drawing board, but by adding a whole series of new adaptations to an existing model, and almost any activity of the brain involves coordination between many (typically up to 20 or 30) areas within the brain. This means that those circuits which handle ancient instincts like competition and aggression almost always work closely with more recently evolved parts which do the thinking and planning, and yet other parts by which we intuit deeper truths and steer our way through apparent jungles of complexity. So there is continuous dialogue between ancient instincts and newer, more open-ended circuitry in the engine rooms below conscious experience.

There is a sense in this of a long-term human agenda still being played out. Perhaps human nature is still incomplete.

Perhaps it has still to finish the implications of its recent evolution and live out the full potential which has been, as it were, written into that evolution. Jesus' teaching about an inner Kingdom, born in us yet still awaiting the day when it could finally transform human society, resonates quite closely with this way of understanding ourselves as an unfinished species.

Jesus points to childhood as one key to the new self-understanding which his inner Kingdom can bring us. Compared to any other species our brain is prodigious, and it also needs time to develop, and for both reasons we are born some years before it reaches its eventual size and a long time indeed before it reaches its full potential in mature adulthood. This means that we have a highly sensitive, imaginative intelligence combined with the longest period of immature dependency, as a proportion of our lifespan, of any animal. This gives us a memory of childhood, celebrated in innumerable ways in our culture, which never fails to fascinate and charm us. But it also gives us much of the inbuilt insecurity which is never far from us for the rest of our lives, the very insecurity which Jesus puts his finger on with such telling and uncomfortable accuracy.

Let's not fall for any delusions. Things may well get worse before they get better. Still, maybe the present age of affluence and insecurity and obsession with consuming things will eventually give way to a cooler, wiser, gentler civilization which at last will develop some kind of realistic, more sophisticated understanding of its own nature and its own ultimate needs. Perhaps we are, after all, hard-wired for transcendence and for self-understanding, emerging in due time in human evolution and bringing with it the liberation of a long pent-up creativity. Can we even dare to hope that this will start to happen before the end of this new century?

Can Jesus' vision of a Kingdom, a source of strength, courage and vision within us, yet inspire us to come home to the flowering of our true potential as the 'wise human'? This is dauntingly uncertain. This could even turn out to be the biggest story of our times and the supreme challenge set for the entire human race. We are children of this sacred place, and our destiny is neither greed nor fear nor violence but the weaving of one world community in which understanding, creativity, beauty, compassion and cooperation can be celebrated in a thousand new ways.

Is this even halfway realistic? That depends on us. More specifically, it depends on the vision we have of our nature, and how clearly we understand our own deepest needs.

Chapter 21
The Man who Cracked the Human Code

At this point we probably need to disentangle ourselves one more time from the assumptions of later history and just remember the man who started all this. Fortunately we have the four remarkable narrative records remembered and set down in the late first century. In their time, with all their human flaws and their unconscious candor, they asserted their memory of Jesus in the context of a rising new theology which saw him as a cosmic figure, increasingly far removed from the man whom some had known as a personal friend.

In our time, we see him through the distorting glass of 20 intervening centuries in which this cosmic picture triumphed, and the resulting travesty which this has left us with (outlined in Chapters 1 and 2) is quite reasonably dismissed by many people today. But these four narrative records, written before the doctrinal certainties of following centuries and later preserved in the aspic of Christian scripture, reveal a first-century figure who can still take us by surprise. The surprises, moreover, are not incidental. They do go to the heart of the story.

Most basically and perhaps reassuringly, the four biblical narratives very deliberately reveal to us a human being like the rest of us, who learns from experience as we do. This man laughs and cries, teases people, likes a bit of good food and good company, but sometimes gets fed up with the crowds. He is convulsed with grief at the unexpected death of Lazarus, and he knows the cold sweat of visceral fear through the long hours of the night before his trial. His ordinary fallible humanity still comes through with remarkable candor and freshness in the details of some of the stories. For example, he seems indulgent to Mary when she sits at his feet meekly listening to him, but surely a bit harsh on her sister Martha, who has only been hard at work preparing the meal! (Does this remind you of any young man you know today?!)

People forget that the Jesus recorded in these narratives is really still quite a young man, and this too is brought out in several passages. His mother comes after him, worrying about him, and he seems dismissive, not to say rude in his response to the concern she shows for him in public and in front of his friends. (Again an amusingly vivid cameo of a young man, wouldn't you say?!) The urgency and certainty and the uncompromising nature of his vision all speak of his youth, as does the frequent directness and lack of diplomacy in his manner of speaking. The temptations in the desert can be seen as a rite of passage, the struggle of a young man to find his destiny. Later, his raw courage and what some no doubt saw as his intemperance in finally taking on the Roman authorities seem to speak of the intensity and utter confidence of youth.

Some of us might prefer to forget, however, just how disreputable this young man is. He eats and drinks with the lowest of the low, the casualties and the marginalized. He seems to be comfortable in the company of people who live a chaotic, insecure existence, shut out from respectable society and living from one day to another. These details have been picked out and emphasized in the narratives, and when their implications dawn on us today they can still shock us. Jesus' teaching is apparently influenced by his daily closeness to this underclass, exhorting all of us to live in trust each day at a time as they do, and to use the experience of each day to build this strong loving bond of trust with our creator within us. As some of this underclass had discovered, this crucial relationship of trust is more precious than anything else we could ever experience because it gives us a new status like no other and a peace independent of the vagaries of existence. Amazingly, this is a lesson from the destitute and the down-and-outs, and this teacher invites the rest of us to take it seriously and apply it to our own lives!

This man has a style and a way of thinking which are unmistakable and highly individual. He meditates on his own tradition with a fearless kind of creativity. We easily forget just how strikingly imaginative his ideas can be – calling for us to be born a second time, for example, or seeing the special status of those whom the rest of us barely notice, or seeing a Kingdom within the heart which is almost like a negative of the everyday world. These are great leaps of the imagination, yet he has the extraordinary skill to see these new realities within a framework of familiar inherited ideas. In his own way, he manages to be conservative yet revolutionary at one and the same time.

In the relatively short period described in the Gospel narratives, he deepens this vision in what seems like one continuous learning curve as he integrates the logic of the political struggle and its talk of a Kingdom, with the very different experience of healing the inner world of the distressed and the disturbed. Eventually he arrives at his central, highly innovative vision, fusing these two different worlds and in the process redefining much of the entire vocabulary and logic of the faith of his ancestors.

Time after time, people struggle to understand what he is talking about. Yet characteristically he doesn't pronounce some final absolute doctrine. He doesn't seem to be interested in definitions. He invites his hearers to see the world in new ways and then to change the way they live – not to believe him in their heads but to follow him. As we saw in a previous chapter, he uses words to intrigue and to challenge rather than to define or analyze, and all the time he interweaves his words with dramatic actions. Instinctively he sees that although words can guide and inspire, actions do speak louder and do matter more in the end.

What drives him to go against the flow like this? Part of it maybe comes from his family tradition (we are told that the family had connections with the Jerusalem temple[107]) and from early expectations of him after the very special circumstances of his birth. His mother seems to have been something of a thinker and prophet in her own right,[108] and her firstborn seems to have been what we would now call a religious prodigy. Luke's single account of him at twelve years old in the temple shows the characteristic intensity and perhaps naivety which would become evident later. [109] Many years later this intensity of focus seems to come to fruition when he experiences an intimate presence within himself which he identifies with the God of Israel. It seems to be the sense of this presence which fires him to live with his characteristic creativity and fearlessness.

At the same time, and this somehow fits in with his creativity, his thinking is very largely undogmatic. He heals, yes, but so do others, and later he prepares his followers to do the same. So it appears that he does not take his healing skills as a sign that he is uniquely divine – this again is the point of view of other people in later times. He accepts that his God does work in similar fashion through other people, urging us to judge him and the others by the same obvious yardstick: the fruits of what they do.

This undogmatic simplicity and practicality is not a side issue either. The writers of the Gospels evidently thought it was important, for they frequently contrast Jesus with others who are forever preoccupied with the details and the niceties of belief, perpetually obsessed with the wild goose chase of human perfection. These are, of course, the Pharisees, with whom Jesus seems at times to be in constant dispute. Some Bible commentators have presented the Pharisees as typical of what was wrong with specifically Jewish attitudes of his own time, but this picture is clearly a bit of a caricature. From what we now know of the Pharisees, Jesus was actually quite close to them in many of his teachings.

It does seem likely that the Pharisees depicted in the narratives were living examples of the extremely conservative, at root perhaps fearful mindset which Jesus himself so berated. Indeed, looking back today, the unconscious reference in these late first-century narratives to a later church's preoccupation with the intricacies of doctrinal dispute is surely hugely ironical and amusing, is it not?

In telling contrast to the Pharisees, so much of Jesus' own teaching comes back to the need for this leap of trust. Time after time he tells people it's their own faith which has healed them, yet almost equally frequently we hear him exclaim to one assembled company after another – apparently in naive, frustrated surprise – how little faith they have! Trust is crucial, but his frustration at people's lack of trust keeps breaking through.

Yes, this young man is quite possibly a touch naive in places, like many visionaries, because he is so absorbed in the extraordinary vision he has got hold of. Yet at the same time, he is becoming experienced at observing human nature in all its variety at close quarters. He has also by now assembled a remarkable range of skills. He is a healer in a known folk tradition of his time and he handles a crowd with a high degree of assurance. He is a talented storyteller with a quick sense of humor and a taste for graphic illustration. He likes to make people smile. He mocks hypocrites and goes out of his way to bring acceptance to outcasts of all kinds. This is a man in whom many talents are beginning to combine, and it's not hard to see why people are drawn to him.

In other words, Jesus has his own natural authority, an authority which, it seems, has nothing to do with the supernatural or that he just happened to be part of God – that, once again, is the hindsight logic of later centuries. Can we still sense something of this original authority today, across the barriers of culture and time? I think we can, because there is a universal appeal to his teaching which can reach us despite its complex roots in the specific culture of his own time. Quite simply, he paints a picture of the human condition which still hits a number of nails on the head. Today we can still recognize the unflinching way in which he sees right through our contradictions and speaks directly to a tender spot deep inside us. We can still feel this searching authority when we reflect on the simple yet extraordinarily radical nature of the promise and the challenge which he offers us. It can still startle us to realize that his tantalizing promise might actually represent for us the completion of our unfinished human nature, the resolution of a contradiction deep within us. This is perhaps why it brings its characteristic exhilaration, an experience of life altogether more energetic and more abundant.

And the challenge? He brushes aside our professions of devotion! His challenge is quite simply to get off our backsides, to seize this opportunity and to make this inner Kingdom actually come alive within us. This seems to be like the kind of challenge which most of us face sooner or later, a challenge to learn a certain wisdom, in the end to mature and to discover who we are. This can indeed be like growing up out of an unfinished adolescence and into a fuller, often somewhat belated human adulthood.

Yet time after time, we find ourselves instinctively trying to avoid this challenge, do we not? And this is the point; this is the nub of the whole thing. This man has hit a nerve inside us. It's as if he has checkmated us into facing the emotional logic of our own human condition, this longing for security which seems to be the price of intelligent self-awareness.

So we respond to him, and hesitate, and turn and think again, all despite ourselves. We feel the urge to run from him, yet we are drawn by an intimation deep within us: the possibility of a great, radiating beauty. Jesus has put his finger on a contradiction and a dilemma and a deep yearning at the very heart of human nature. This is an extraordinary achievement, surely the very source of his natural authority and ultimately of his claim to historical greatness.

What was it that so moved and so fired him? What was the key? The narrative portrays him withdrawing frequently to the solitude of the hills, seeking out times of stillness, alternating with times when he is surrounded by people. Kahlil Gibran's prose catches an impression of this.

> In every aspect of the day Jesus was aware of the Father. He beheld him in the clouds and in the shadows of the clouds that pass over the earth. He saw the Father's face reflected in the quiet pools, and in the faint print of his feet in the sand ... The night spoke to him with the voice of the Father, and in solitude he heard the angel of the Lord calling to him. And when he stilled himself to sleep, he heard the whispering of the heavens in his dreams.[110]

For some, the language here is maybe over-romanticized, but nevertheless the key to the whole enigma of Jesus, and the appeal of his invitation to us, lies perhaps right here, in the overwhelming beauty of this relationship of trust. This is what Jesus called the pearl of great price, and just occasionally we can recognize that we would give anything to gain this trust, if only we dared. This haunting desire of the heart, this childhood dream of coming home, this very elixir of life which can break down the walls of the ego, still our fears and set us free – this is his epic discovery. And once it's out, you can't put it back in the box; you can't un-discover it.

At last the human code has been cracked and the greatest of all the puzzles of life begins to make a kind of sense. The beauty of life leaps out at us, hope comes alive, and suddenly we are given a reason to celebrate, a reason to dance. This perhaps is his real legacy to all of us, echoing within human hearts down the centuries.

Appendix
The Logic of Trinity

It took a remarkably long time to arrive at a consensus on the Christian doctrine of the Trinity. Behind this, we can perhaps discern a final weakening of Jewish influence within this increasingly Greek faith as it continued to spread now more rapidly across the eastern Mediterranean world and then into Italy, Africa and the far provinces of the western empire, into the Gothic kingdoms in the north across the Danube, and into Armenia and Persia to the east. It was perhaps also the expression of a maturing, increasingly self-confident Christian community, and the slow emergence of a canon of Christian scripture and the three-tier authority structure of bishop, priest and deacon.

The particular understanding of the Trinity which was finally achieved expresses a moment in late classical Greek culture, still enthusiastically immersed in word debates inherited from a dazzling philosophical tradition. Formulae of words recited in churches to this day, like 'begotten not made' or 'very God of very God', still encode long-forgotten disputes from this foreign world. Perhaps we need to unpack something of what it meant to people then, if we are to make any kind of sense in it now.

Everywhere We Look
The idea of trinity is far from unique to Christianity; in fact trinities have arisen repeatedly in human history. Hinduism has the trinity of Brahma, Vishnu and Shiva, or God the creator, sustainer and destroyer-transformer, together dancing the dance of the sacred universe, and this maybe gives us a clue as to why an apparently strange idea like trinity arises. How do we sum up our creation, our entire reality, in one word? Quite simply, a vast

conception like a monotheistic God has such widely different aspects – if you like, different jobs to do.

Sufi Islam in time produced *islam*, *iman* and *ihsan*, that is (as I understand it), surrender to God's will, inner experience of God's presence, and outward integrity expressing this experience in daily life. Buddhism, formally an agnostic system, eventually came upon Buddha, dharma and sangha: the teacher, the teaching and the community of followers. Buddhism has a further trinity in its model of ideal human learning, involving understanding, compassion and action, each in turn liberating the other two until they achieve the eventual supreme harmony of enlightenment.

In various mystical traditions the number three reconciles the many and the one, the teeming multitude of reality and its ultimate unity. Others have pointed to the three coordinates in the dimension of space, and to the three phases, if that's the right word, to the mysterious arrow of time: past, present and future. Plato divided the human soul into three: the intellect, the emotions and the will (and also divides his ideal society into three classes), and this echoes the later Christian understanding of the threefold essence of humanity in body, soul and spirit.

Somewhat later, Augustine of Hippo meditated on the threefold mind of God and stumbled on to a threefold understanding of the human mind itself, coming close to the idea of an unconscious many centuries before Freud's id, ego and superego. In the mid-twentieth century came a triune model of the brain, recapitulating our long evolution with its reptilian, mammalian and hominid brain, located broadly in the brain stem, limbic system and neocortex respectively.

But it was the second-century neo-Pythagorean philosopher Numenius who formulated a pagan trinity startlingly close to the eventual Christian formulation.[111] The ultimate God was, first, the unfathomable mystery of existence, something beyond all categories or descriptions in words. The second aspect was the creative rational power involved in the world of becoming, similar to the Logos. Finally, the third aspect was God alive within all people and all things, recalling the Stoic idea of world-soul, an idea in some ways reminiscent of the Holy Spirit.

Numenius, too, had predecessors. Philo of Alexandria, a Jewish philosopher whose work brought together Jewish and Greek thought, was saying something not unlike this during or shortly after Jesus' own lifetime. It may be from Philo that John took the idea of the Word, the Logos, which was both an agent of God and in a way an aspect of God. Likewise Numenius could possibly have got his ideas from Plato, or from Philo, or indeed from John, or direct from Stoic writing. Thinkers both Christian and non-Christian were trying to span the chasm between the unifying rational force in the creation and the teeming multiplicity of the world of things, and time and again came on the idea of trinity to express this.

Jesus, too, although in no sense himself a Trinitarian, was thinking very much in the same problem area: how to bring the transforming otherness of the creator of all things right in among us.

A Christian Trinity Emerges

For early Christians, the starting point was the puzzle and the wonder of Jesus' startling new teaching. God the father of Israel was now translated into Abba, the intimate presence within the heart of every one of us. The idea of the Holy Spirit derived from antecedents in Jewish Wisdom writing. By bringing these two innovations together, Jesus created a new understanding of a God among us, not only passionate about our welfare but dynamically active within and around us. These were transforming innovations, and for a time in the second and third centuries it seemed that the eventual consensus might rest there.

But the awareness that Jesus himself had been the revealer of all this, and the memory of his deeds and his words preserved in the four Gospels, led to a growing feeling that he must have been more than just the messenger. John's account in particular shows a Jesus uniquely confident of a special closeness to God. In the words of the writer of the epistle to the Hebrews, he was the author and finisher of the faith. It was Jesus who had created this whole new world, this new way of seeing our humanity.

It does seem clear from what we understand of Jewish belief of the time that it would have been perfectly natural for Jesus to feel called to be the messenger of God. He could have felt at one with this presence of Abba within, and he could even have felt called to demonstrate his remarkable new vision of the passionate, self-forgetting nature of this God. But would it have even crossed his mind to see himself as a constitutive part of his God, or as in any way co-equal with him? Wouldn't he have been horrified at such presumption? 'Why do you call me good? No one is good except God alone.'[112] His humility before his God was deeply characteristic. Besides, these were recognizably Greek ideas (Greeks were among his close neighbors in Galilee). Greek gods were like superhuman creatures, but the Jewish understanding was of a God who was sovereign in ways radically unlike any of his creatures.

At the same time, it perhaps began to dawn on Jesus that he had to challenge the power of the kingdoms of this world directly and not just in words. This seemed to fit the idea of the suffering servant described in his scriptures, a servant-leader whose suffering could move people and galvanize them into a change of heart. Perhaps he was being led to enact that very special role, and become that special servant of God himself. So it does seem that everything arises from Jesus' developing understanding of his own role. But it would take his followers a long time to arrive at a systematic understanding.

True, there are several passages in the New Testament which seem to come close to a Trinitarian view of the role of Jesus. Right at the end of Matthew's Gospel, the terms Father, Son and Holy

Spirit are mentioned together for the first time in the same breath.[113] Others would say that an isolated text like this is unrepresentative of thinking at the time, and may indeed bear the hallmark of a later addition to the text. In John's later account, Thomas also does address Jesus as 'My Lord and my God[114]', but thinking of the time more typically describes Jesus as a great servant raised up by God, a great prophet, comparing him to Moses or Elijah, for instance.

Other places in the New Testament accounts are perhaps more typical of late first-century ways of thinking, where words are used which strain to express the inexpressible – words like the wisdom of God, the light which lights everyone, the reflection of God's glory, and the exact imprint of God's very being. Unambiguous Trinitarian doctrines came a long time later.

Paul is sometimes seen as an early Trinitarian, his great benediction to the Corinthians being quoted in support of this: 'The grace of the Lord Jesus Christ, and the love of God, and the fellowship of the Holy Spirit, be with you all.'[115] This does have a Trinitarian feel about it, but looking closer, in Paul's formulation the idea of God the Father is not used – perhaps it was not yet in current usage. Jesus is clearly Lord in the daily life of his followers; and the living presence, the fellowship, of the Holy Spirit is confirmed. But God in Paul's blessing does seem in some way separate and unique. This view apparently fits the broader picture of how people seem to have thought in the first century.

A good deal of the time, the early Trinitarian debate seemed to circle around the relationship of Jesus with God the Father. The role and status of the Holy Spirit, having enjoyed such early prominence after the Pentecost experience, apparently lagged behind for much of the time in the following centuries. Perhaps it was too anarchic and personal, and didn't fit easily within the growing hierarchical thinking of the period. Apparently it wasn't until the first Council of Constantinople, as late as 381 CE, that the Holy Spirit was unambiguously declared to be part of the

Trinity, not just an emissary of God.

By late classical times, one more final change was taking place. Early theology had pictured Jesus as uniquely close to God but clearly subject to him – his servant, in fact – raised up by God with special authority. John has Jesus say, 'The Father is greater than I am.'[116] Indeed it was his obedience and subjection to the will of God which had marked Jesus out. At the Council of Chalcedon in 451, by contrast, Jesus is finally declared the co-equal of God the Father, confirming a crucial shift from the earlier understanding. The doctrine of the Trinity in its late classical form had finally been established.

However, by this time another change was taking place. Jesus' own remarkable vision of God was being increasingly replaced by an earlier understanding in the minds of many ex-pagan Christian converts. For the emperor Constantine and for many others, God had become once again the war god of the pagans, and Jesus therefore was like his lieutenant. In time, God and his Son had become so august and distant that Mary and all the saints were required to mediate for poor helpless humankind. Access to the Father and the Son had become the prerogative of a whole hierarchy of priestly gatekeepers.

Seeing Jesus in this way robbed him of the last vestiges of his humanity. If the new public faith required an exaggerated obeisance before him, very much as you would make to a despotic ruler, this would have the effect of removing him from any public discussion or debate. In time it became a heinous offense, justifying a display of great public anger, to call his status into question in any way. This put authority into the hands of a hierarchy and its leaders, and very soon it became an equal offense to question them either, for were they not God's authorized deputies? In this way the faith of Jesus was carried forward and proclaimed, but in a darker form, with stress on atonement, sacrifice, human unworthiness ... and control.

It hardly needs to be said that today this authoritarian, establishment view of the Trinity is still widely influential, firmly lodged in our unconscious after all these centuries. Doesn't this view need to be thoroughly shaken out of mainstream Christian belief? Doesn't it cut across the Kingdom teaching of Jesus pretty comprehensively?

Trinity and Us

Some would maintain that the doctrine of the Trinity was at root really little more than a Greek form of words, making a quintessentially Greek sense of Jesus' original teaching. In the fourth century the so-called Cappadocian fathers (Basil, Gregory of Nyssa and Gregory of Naziansus, who worked in Cappadocia, a Roman province now situated in central Turkey) had finally arrived at an adequate form of words to achieve this. Their view sees God as the single essence and sacred wonder of our total Reality, and the Trinity as the three *energeia* or channels through which this Reality interacts with human experience in the Christian gospel. (I hope this short summation in modern words does justice to the full idea.)

People today have a picture of God consisting of three persons, in unity together but at the same time three distinct persons in an eternal, pre-existing Trinity. But this recipe for confusion does seem to have arisen from a fateful early ambiguity in the original Latin word *persona* (and its Greek original *prosopon*). Three *personae* apparently doesn't have to mean three 'persons' in the modern sense of three individuals, but can equally mean three masks or three faces, like the energeia of the Cappadocian fathers. This understanding is surely simpler and more convincing, is it not?

Quite incidentally, it does also seem somewhat closer to Jewish and Muslim ways of picturing God, who is one but has many names, and not too distant from the Hindu pantheon, in which all the gods are avatars (or personae, we could almost say) of one God. More importantly, though, this simpler understanding of the Trinity authentically reflects back Jesus' own teaching. Jesus enacts in himself this ego-less creator who is alive within all his creation and from his own infinite creativity continuously gives himself away. That's the bit that matters, isn't it, more than the precise status of personhood within the Trinity?

Today some people are happy to assent to a belief in the traditional Trinity, believing that its very strangeness in some way helps to express the strange mystery of our existence. For others, the Trinity simply expresses Jesus' message that God is among us. However, many Christian people today, although they see no particular problem in assenting to the doctrine of the Trinity, don't really find it much of a living inspiration in their faith either. This doctrine is no longer self-evident. For many people its power to illuminate and inspire has faded.

The Brazilian Leonardo Boff sees in the doctrine of the Trinity an echo of three tendencies which he sees in human society: 'upward', 'outward' and 'inward' tendencies which ideally need to achieve some kind of balance. Another theologian, John Haught, refers to the Christian Trinity as an 'eternal divine drama', expressing nothing less than the dynamic rhythm of life, death and resurrection (or rebirth) underlying the entire created universe. At first sight these attempts to rethink the meaning of trinity for today appear to be trying to shoehorn an old doctrine to fit new perceptions, apparently in an attempt to salvage a way of thinking which maybe no longer speaks naturally to our own times.

The formulation of trinity by the neo-Pythagorean Numenius may be worth restating here precisely because of its philosophical clarity. There is God the magnificent mystery of our whole creation; God the rational principle behind the world of becoming; and the living God who indwells every single created thing and every one of us. The Christian Trinity in some ways echoes this splendid vision but it cannot match its elegant, concise comprehensiveness. Indeed the Numenius version may be for some a clearer reformulation of trinity specifically for today.

The Christian Trinity, though, was never intended as an elegant philosophical formulation, but as a way of understanding the teaching of Jesus, and this teaching adds a vital dimension which Numenius misses entirely. In Numenius there is no therapy, no antidote to the exile of the human heart. The God Jesus saw is an overwhelmingly generous, self-giving, self-forgetting presence within us, and this can inspire us, take us right out of ourselves, and save us from our headless, fearful ego. This teaching of Jesus will stand the test of time whether people understand it in Trinitarian terms or not. It speaks to the heart. Is this not the very core of his gospel?

Notes

1 Luke 15:11–14, 17–24

2 C.F.Alexander, 'Once in Royal David's City', 1848

3 For example in E.P. Saunders, *The Historical Figure of Jesus*, Penguin, 1996

4 Luke 1:1–4

5 Geza Vermes, *Jesus the Jew*, Collins, 1973. Vermes himself was born a Jew, educated as a Christian, and returned later in life to his Jewish roots.

6 Keith Akers, *The Lost Religion of Jesus*, Lantern Books, 2000

7 Acts 6:8 – 8:1

8 Robert Funk and Roy Hoover, *The Five Gospels: The Search for the Authentic Words of Jesus*, Macmillan, 1993

9 See in David Boulton, *Who on Earth was Jesus? The Modern Quest for the Jesus of History*, O Books, 2008

10 See in Josef Ratzinger, *Jesus of Nazareth*, Bloomsbury, 2007

11 See the article on Homer by Dennis Ronald MacDonald in Leslie Houlden (ed.), *Jesus in History, Thought and Culture*, ABC Clio, 2003

12 Gerald O'Collins, *Jesus: A Portrait*, Darton, Longman and Todd, 2008, and Richard Bauckham, *Jesus and the Eyewitnesses*, Eerdmans, 2008

13 1 Corinthians 9:5

14 See, for example, in John Henson, *The Gay Disciple*, O Books, 2008

15 John 9:1–7

16 Margaret Barker, *Christmas: The Original Story*, SPCK, 2008

17 See Anselm Grün, *Jesus the Image of Humanity: Luke's Account*, Continuum, 2003

18 I am indebted in this section to Richard Buckner, *The Joy of Jesus: Humour in the Gospels*, The Canterbury Press, 1993

19 Luke 7:31–34

20 Luke 14:4–6, alternative reading

21 Matthew 15:14

22 Luke 18:24–25; also featured in Matthew's and Mark's accounts – clearly a favorite story!

23 Matthew 6:2

24 Matthew 5:14–15; also Luke 8:16

25 Mark 7:18–19; also Matthew 15:17

26 Matthew 22:15–22

27 Luke 7:37–50

28 Marcus Borg, *Meeting Jesus Again for the First Time*, HarperCollins, 1994

29 John 3:1–12

30 See Matthew 5:1–13 and Luke 6:20–26 for intriguingly different versions

31 Luke 2:41–51

32 Matthew 4:1–11; Luke 4:1–13

33 For example in Mark 3:20–27; Luke 11:14–20

34 For example in Mark 8:11–13. It's true that in John's account Jesus performs miracles to show his divine power, but in the other three narratives he is more reluctant to do this.

35 Matthew 27:42–43; Mark 15:31–32; Luke 23:35–36

36 Antonia Swinson, *Root of All Evil?* Saint Andrew Press, 2003

37 Pocket World in Figures, *The Economist*, 2009

38 2 Corinthians 8:9

39 Matthew 6:19

40 Matthew 6:24

41 Matthew 19:16–22; Mark 10:17–22

42 Matthew 6:21

43 See in Josef Ratzinger, *Jesus of Nazareth*, Bloomsbury, 2007

44 Matthew 21:1–9

45 Matthew 27:17

46 Luke 23:19

47 Matthew 13:45–46

48 Luke 12:27–28

49 Sometimes 'Give us this day our daily bread' is rendered 'Give us bread enough for today'.

50 Luke 19:1–10

51 Mark 12:28–31. The Shema starts with the words 'Hear, O Israel: the Lord our God, the Lord is one'.

52 With acknowledgements to Michael Adam, *Wandering in Eden*, Wildwood House, 1973

53 In Dorin Barter, *Grace Abounding*, Darton, Longman and Todd, 1993

54 In John Michael Mountney, *Sin Shall Be a Glory*, Darton, Longman and Todd, 1992

55 Matthew 5:38–41 and Luke 6:29, elucidated in Walter Wink, *The Powers that Be*, Doubleday, 1998

56 Hebrews 5.8

57 John A.T. Robinson, *The Human Face of God*, SCM Press, 1973

58 In *Jesus the Jew*, Collins, 1973 and also mentioned in David Boulton, *Who on Earth was Jesus?* O Books, 2008

59 For example in Mark 16:10–11

60 Mark 15.34

61 Recorded in all four narratives, for example in Matthew 27:35

62 Luke 24:13–32

63 Isaiah 53.4 (Authorized Version)

64 1 Corinthians 15:12–19

65 Acts 2:27; Peter is quoting Psalm 16:10

66 Matthew 27:19

67 In *Did Jesus Die?* produced by Planet Wild and shown on BBC4 on 1 May 2006. The sponge is mentioned in John 19:28–30.

68 Dr Roger James, in a letter to a recent edition of the *London Review of Books*

69 John 20:24–29

70 Geza Vermes, *The Resurrection*, (Penguin, 2008)

71 In H.A. Williams, *True Resurrection*, Collins, 1983

72 Mark 16:19; Luke 24:50–51; Acts 1:9–11

73 See in Paul William Roberts, *The Journey of the Magi*, Anansi, 1995

74 Alfred H. Ackley, 'He lives', 1933

75 John 10.30

76 See in Mark Tully, *An Investigation into the Lives of Jesus*, Penguin/BBC, 1996

77 Matthew 25:34–40

78 Albert Schweitzer, *The Quest of the Historical Jesus1906*

79 Isaiah 7:14, quoted again in Matthew 1:23

80 Matthew 3:16–17

81 Luke 3:1–2

82 Luke 1:27

83 A more detailed account of this can be found in Geza Vermes, *The Nativity: History and Legend*, Penguin, 2006

84 Ibid.

85 Charles Wesley, 'Hark! The Herald Angels Sing', 1739

86 Acts 1:6

87 See in Gerd Theissen and Annette Merz, *The Historical Jesus*; also in Keith Akers, *The Lost Religion of Jesus*

88 Acts 6:8 – 7:53

89 See in Kamal Salibi, *Who Was Jesus?* I.B. Tauris, 1992 and Reza Aslan, *No God but God*, Arrow Books, 2006

90 Paul William Roberts, *Journey of the Magi*, Anansi, 1995

91 See the article on Homer in Jesus in Leslie Houlden (ed.), *History, Thought and Culture*, ABC Clio, 2003

92 See Paul Kriwaczek, *In Search of Zarathustra*, Weidenfeld and Nicholson, 2002

93 See Charles Freeman, *The Closing of the Western Mind*, Pimlico, 2003

94 1 Timothy 6:10–12

95 Galatians 3:28–29

96 See in Alister McGrath, *Dawkins' God*, Blackwell, 2005 and in John Haught, *Christianity and Science*, Orbis Books, 2007

97 Quoted in Alister McGrath, *Dawkins' God*, Blackwell, 2005

98 Jürgen Moltmann, 'Hope and History', *Theology Today* 25, 1968

99 Robin Dunbar, 'We believe: An evolutionary biologist's view',

New Scientist, 28 January 2006, and Michael Brooks, 'Natural born believers', *New Scientist*, 7 February 2009

100 See article by Peter Forster in Leslie Houlden (ed.), *Jesus in History, Thought and Culture*, ABC Clio, 2003

101 Brian Swimme, *The Universe is a Green Dragon*, Bear and Co, 1984

102 For example, Martin Rees, *Our Final Century: The 50/50 Threat to Humanity's Survival*, Heinemann, 2003

103 Malvina Reynolds, 'Magic Penny', 1986

104 See in Dan Jones, 'Humanity's greatest journey: Tracing a new route out of Africa', *New Scientist*, 27 October 2007, and Stephen Oppenheimer, *Out of Eden: The Peopling of the World*, Eerdmans, 2008

105 Jürgen Moltmann, 'Hope and History', *Theology Today* 25, 1968

106 As reported in 'The population delusion: Seven billion and counting', *New Scientist*, 26 September 2009

107 Luke 1:5–7

108 Luke 1:46–55

109 Luke 2:41–51

110 From 'John the beloved disciple in his old age' in Kahlil Gibran, *Jesus the Son of Man*, Oneworld, 1993

111 See in Emily Hunt, *Christianity in the Second Century: The Case of Tatian*, Routledge, 2003

112 Mark 10:18; also Matthew 19:17; Luke 18:19

113 Matthew 28:18–20

114 John 20.28

115 2 Corinthians 13:14

116 John 14:28

Sources

The following books and articles have influenced the writing of this book. Some have been read recently, others some years back. Some have contributed to significant points of detail; others have influenced a wider range of ideas. Some are concerned specifically with Jesus, others with the wider perspectives within which I believe we need to understand Jesus today.

Adam, Michael, *Wandering in Eden: Three Ways to the East within Us*, Wildwood House, 1973

Akers, Keith, *The Lost Religion of Jesus*, Lantern Books, 2000

Ambler, Rex, *Light to Live By*, Quaker Books, 2002

Anderson, Walt, *Open Secrets: A Western Guide to Tibetan Buddhism*, Penguin, 1979

Armstrong, John, *Conditions of Love: The Philosophy of Intimacy*, Penguin, 2002

Armstrong, Karen, *A History of God: From Abraham to the Present*, Heinemann, 1993

Armstrong, Karen, *The Great Transformation: The World in the Time of Buddha, Socrates, Confucius and Jeremiah*, Atlantic Books, 2006

Armstrong, Karen, *The Bible: The Biography*, Atlantic Books, 2007

Aslan, Reza, *No God but God: The Origins, Evolution and Future of Islam*, Arrow Books, 2006

Barbour, Ian, *When Science Meets Religion: Enemies, Strangers or Partners?* SPCK, 2000

Barclay, William, *The Mind of Jesus*, SCM Press, 1960

Barker, Gregory A. (ed.), *Jesus in the World's Faiths: Thinkers from Five Religions Reflect on His Meaning*, Orbis, 2005

Barter, Dorin, *Grace Abounding: Wrestling with Sin and Guilt*, Darton, Longman and Todd, 1993

Bauckham, Richard, *The Theology of Jürgen Moltmann*, T&T Clark, 1995

Beattie, Tina, *The New Atheists: The Twilight of Reason and the War on Religion*, Darton, Longman and Todd, 2007

Blamires, David (ed.), *What Jesus Means to Me: 19 Friends Speaking Personally*, Friends' Quarterly/Woodbrooke Quaker Study Centre, 2003

Boff, Leonardo, *Trinity and Society*, Burns and Oates, 1988

Borg, Marcus, *Meeting Jesus Again for the First Time: The Historical Jesus and the Heart of Contemporary Faith*, HarperCollins, 1994

Borg, Marcus, *The God We Never Knew: Beyond Dogmatic Religion to a More Authentic Contemporary Faith*, HarperSanFrancisco, 1997

Borg, Marcus and John Dominic Crossan, *The Last Week: What the Gospels Really Teach about Jesus' Final Days in Jerusalem*, HarperCollins, 2006

Boulton, David, *Who on Earth was Jesus? The Modern Quest for the Jesus of History*, O Books, 2008

Bowden, John, *Jesus: The Unanswered Questions*, SCM Press, 1988

Brooks, Michael, 'Natural born believers', *New Scientist*, 7 February 2009

Browning, W.R.F., *Dictionary of the Bible*, Oxford, 1996

Buckner, Richard, *The Joy of Jesus: Humour in the Gospels*, The Canterbury Press, 1993

Burnell, Jocelyn Bell, *Broken for Life: The 1989 Swarthmore Lecture*, Quaker Home Service, 1989

Campbell, Ken, *Brainspotting: Consciousness, the Self and the Mind*, Channel Four Books, 1996

Chadwick, Henry, *Augustine: A Very Short Introduction*, Oxford, 1986

Chignell, Meg, *The Universal Jesus*, Sessions Book Trust, 1990

Collins, Roger, *Early Medieval Europe 300–1000*, Macmillan, 1991

Cunliffe, Barry (foreword), *Atlas of World History*, Cassell, 1997

Cupitt, Don, *The Debate about Christ*, SCM Press, 1979

Cupitt, Don, *Taking Leave of God*, SCM Press, 1980

Cupitt, Don, *The Sea of Faith: Christianity in Change*, BBC, 1984

Danielson, Dennis Richard (ed.), *The Book of the Cosmos: Imagining the Universe from Heraclitus to Hawking*, Perseus, 2000

Davies, Paul, *The Mind of God: Science and the Search for Ultimate Meaning*, Simon and Schuster, 1992

Dawkins, Richard, *The Blind Watchmaker*, Penguin, 1986

Dunbar, Robin, 'We believe: An evolutionary biologist's view', part of Special Report: Beyond Belief, *New Scientist*, 28 January 2006

The Economist, 'The proper study of mankind: A survey of human evolution', 24 December 2005

The Economist, Pocket World in Figures, 2009

Ehrman, Bart D., *Lost Scriptures: Books that Did Not Make it into the New Testament*, Oxford, 2003

Eyre, Ronald, *The Long Search: His Own Account of a Three-Year Journey*, Collins/BBC, 1979

Fernandez-Armesto, Felipe, *Millennium: A History of Our Last Thousand Years*, QPD, 1995

Finkelstein, Israel and Neil Asher Silberman, *The Bible Unearthed: Archaeology's New Vision of Ancient Israel and the Origin of its Sacred Texts*, Touchstone, 2002

Fortey, Richard, *Life: An Unauthorized Biography*, HarperCollins, 1997

Freeman, Charles, *The Closing of the Western Mind: The Rise of Faith and the Fall of Reason*, Pimlico, 2003

Funk, Robert W. and Roy W. Hoover, *The Five Gospels: The Search for the Authentic Words of Jesus*, Macmillan, 1993

Funk, Robert W., *Honest to Jesus: Jesus for a New Millennium*, HarperCollins, 1996

George, Susan, *Another World is Possible if...*, Verso/Transnational Institute, 2004

Gibran, Kahlil, *Jesus the Son of Man: His Words and His Deeds as Told and Recorded by Those who Knew Him*, Oneworld, 1993

Gordon, Mick and Chris Wilkinson (eds.), *Conversations on Religion*, Continuum, 2008

Gould, Stephen Jay, *Wonderful Life: The Burgess Shale and the Nature of History*, Penguin, 1989

Grayling, C., *What is Good? The Search for the Best Way to Live*,

Phoenix, 2003

Greenfield, Susan ,*The Private Life of the Brain*, Penguin, 2000

Gribbin, John, *Stardust: The Cosmic Recycling of Stars, Planets and People*, Penguin, 2000

Grün, Anselm, *Jesus the Image of Humanity: Luke's Account*, Continuum, 2003

Haught, John F., *Christianity and Science: Towards a Theology of Nature*, Orbis, 2007

Heaney, Seamus and Ted Hughes (editors), *The Rattle Bag*, Faber and Faber, 1982

Holloway, Richard, *Crossfire: Faith and Doubt in an Age of Certainty*, Collins, 1988

Holloway, Richard, *Dancing on the Edge: Faith in a Post-Christian Age*, Fount/Harper Collins, 1997

Holloway, Richard, *On Forgiveness*, Canongate, 2002

Houlden, Leslie (ed.), *Jesus in History, Thought and Culture: An Encyclopedia in Two Volumes*, ABC Clio, 2003

Hunt, Emily J., *Christianity in the Second Century: The Case of Tatian*, Routledge, 2003

Kohn, Marek,*As We Know It: Coming to Terms with an Evolved Mind*, Granta, 1999

Kriwaczek, Paul, *In Search of Zarathustra*, Weidenfeld and Nicolson, 2002

Lampen, John, *Twenty Questions about Jesus*, Quaker Home Service, 1984

Manson, Peter (director), *Did Jesus Die?* a program produced by Planet Wild and shown on BBC4, 1 May 2006

Marsh, Clive and Steve Moyise, *Jesus and the Gospels: An Introduction*, Cassell, 1999

McEvedy, Colin, *Atlas of Ancient History*, Penguin, 1967

McEvedy, Colin, *Atlas of Medieval History*, Penguin, 1961

McGrath, Alister, *Dawkins' God: Genes, Memes and the Meaning of Life*, Blackwell, 2005

Menocal, Maria Rosa, *The Ornament of the World: How Muslims, Jews and Christians Created a Culture of Tolerance in Medieval Spain*, Little, Brown and Co., 2002

Mithen, Steven, *The Prehistory of the Mind: A Search for the Origins of Art, Religion and Science*, Phoenix, 1996

Moltmann, Jürgen, 'Hope in History', *Theology Today* 25, 1968

Mountney, John Michael, *Sin Shall Be a Glory: As Revealed by Julian of Norwich*, Darton, Longman and Todd, 1992

Muggeridge, Malcolm, *Jesus Rediscovered*, Fontana, 1969

Norwich, John Julius, *Byzantium: The Early Centuries*, Penguin, 1988

Nouwen, Henri, *The Return of the Prodigal Son: A Story of Homecoming*, Doubleday, 1992

Oppenheimer, Stephen, *Out of Eden: The Peopling of the World*, Constable and Robinson, 2003

Pagels, Elaine, *The Gnostic Gospels*, Penguin, 1979

Polkinghorne, John, *One World: The Interaction of Science and Theology*, SPCK, 1986

Powell, Mark Allan, *The Jesus Debate: Modern Historians Investigate the Life of Christ*, Lion, 1998

Quaker Faith and Practice: The Book of Christian Discipline of the Yearly Meeting
of the Religious Society of Friends (Quakers) in Britain, 1995

Quaker Quest, *Twelve Quakers and Jesus*, 2007

Ramsey, Michael, *Holy Spirit: A Biblical Study*, SPCK, 1977

Ratzinger, Josef, Pope Benedict XVI, *Jesus of Nazareth*, Bloomsbury/Doubleday, 2007

Rees, Martin, *Just Six Numbers: The Deep Forces that Shape the Universe*, Phoenix, 1999

Richardson, Alan and John Bowden (editors), *A New Dictionary of Christian Theology*, SCM Press, 1983

Robinson, John A.T., *Honest to God*, SCM Press, 1963

Robinson, John A.T., *The Human Face of God*, SCM Press, 1973

Sanders, E.P., *Paul: A Very Short Introduction*, Oxford, 1991

Sanders, E.P., *The Historical Figure of Jesus*, Penguin, 1996

Schulz, Charles, *Peanuts Every Sunday*, Holt, Rinehart and Winston,

1961

Scruton, Roger, 'The sacred and the human', *Prospect*, August 2007

Shah-Kazemi, Reza, *Jesus in the Quran: An Akbari Perspective*, www.ibnarabisociety.org/articles/rezashah.htmi

Smart, Ninian ,*World Religions: A Dialogue*, Penguin, 1960

Soelle, Dorothee and Luise Schottroff, *Jesus of Nazareth*, SPCK, 2002

Swimme, Brian, *The Universe is a Green Dragon*, Bear and Co., 1984

Swinson, Antonia, *Root of All Evil? How to Make Spiritual Values Count*, Saint Andrew Press, 2003

Theissen, Gerd and Annette Merz, *The Historical Jesus: A Comprehensive Guide*, SCM Press, 1998

Thorne, Brian, *Behold the Man: A Therapist's Meditations on the Passion of Jesus Christ*, Darton, Longman and Todd, 1991

Tolle, Eckhart, *Stillness Speaks*, Hodder and Stoughton, 2003

Tully, Mark, *An Investigation into the Lives of Jesus*, Penguin/BBC, 1996

Vanier, Jean, *Becoming Human*, Anansi, 1998

Vermes, Geza, *Jesus the Jew: A Historian's Reading of the Gospels*, Collins, 1973

Vermes, Geza, *The Nativity: History and Legend*, Penguin, 2006

Vermes, Geza, *The Resurrection*, Penguin, 2008

Wakeman, Hilary, *Saving Christianity: New Thinking for Old Beliefs*, The Liffey Press, 2003

Ward, Keith, *Re-thinking Christianity*, Oneworld, 2007

Warner, Marina, *Alone of All Her Sex: The Myth and Cult of the Virgin Mary*, Picador, 1985

Watts, Alan, *Der Lauf des Wassers/The Way of Running Water: An Introduction to Taoism*, Suhrkamp, 1975

Westmorland General Meeting, *Preparing for Peace by Asking the Experts to Analyse War*, Britain Yearly Meeting of the Religious Society of Friends, 2005

Williams, H.A., *True Wilderness*, Constable, 1965

Williams, H.A., *True Resurrection*, Collins, 1983

Williams, Patricia, *Quakerism: A Theology for our Time*, William

Sessions, 2007

Williams, Rowan, *The Wound of Knowledge: Christian Spirituality from the New Testament to St John of the Cross*, Darton, Longman and Todd, 1990

Wink, Walter, *The Powers that Be: Theology for a New Millennium*, Doubleday, 1998

Wright, N.T., *The Challenge of Jesus*, SPCK, 2000

Yancey, Philip, *Soul Survivor: How My Faith Survived the Church*, Hodder and Stoughton, 2001

BOOKS

O is a symbol of the world, of oneness and unity. In different cultures it also means the "eye," symbolizing knowledge and insight. We aim to publish books that are accessible, constructive and that challenge accepted opinion, both that of academia and the "moral majority."

Our books are available in all good English language bookstores worldwide. If you don't see the book on the shelves ask the bookstore to order it for you, quoting the ISBN number and title. Alternatively you can order online (all major online retail sites carry our titles) or contact the distributor in the relevant country, listed on the copyright page.

See our website **www.o-books.net** for a full list of over 500 titles, growing by 100 a year.

And tune in to myspiritradio.com for our book review radio show, hosted by June-Elleni Laine, where you can listen to the authors discussing their books.

MySpiritRadio